/TheVoiceOfFootball | WWW.SHOOT.CO.UK | @_shootfootball

ACTING ANNUAL EDITOR : **Dan Church**

CONTENTS

This Shoot Annual belongs to:

Draw Profile picture:

Birthday:

Position:

Football Club I play for:

Favourite Team:

Favourite Player:

Player Ratings: (out of 5 stars)

Speed: ☆☆☆☆☆

Strength: ☆☆☆☆☆

Passing: ☆☆☆☆☆

Skill: ☆☆☆☆☆

Heading: ☆☆☆☆☆

Crossing: ☆☆☆☆☆

Dribbling: ☆☆☆☆☆

Shooting: ☆☆☆☆☆

Defending: ☆☆☆☆☆

Goalkeeping: ☆☆☆☆☆

Total Stars: __ /50

SHOOT's A to Z of the Premier League

Think you know your ABCs? Well, as we celebrate the 26th Premier League season, *SHOOT* has created an alphabetical index of things to look forward to during the 2017-18 campaign...

A = Awards

Dele Alli was named the PFA Young Player of the Year for the second successive year last season. Can the midfield maestro win the award for a third time this term?

B = Brighton and Hove Albion

The Seagulls will be playing in the top-flight of English football for the first time since 1983. Brighton nearly dropped down into non-league football just 20 years ago!

C = Champions League spots

The best of the best battle it out for a top four finish and subsequent qualification for the UEFA Champions League.

D = Diving

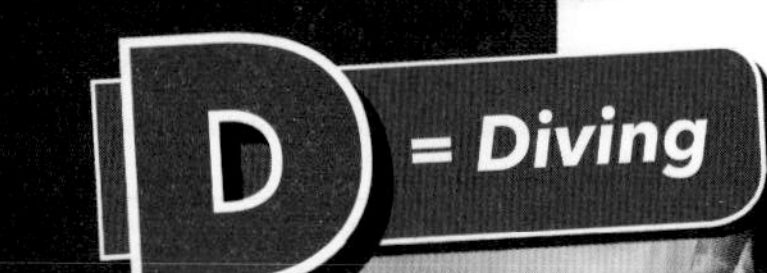

One of the biggest problems in the beautiful game. But I suppose we can let the goalkeepers off!

E = European embarrassment

Both Arsenal and Manchester City were emphatically dumped out of the UEFA Champions League Round of 16 last season. Tottenham didn't even make it out of the group stage!

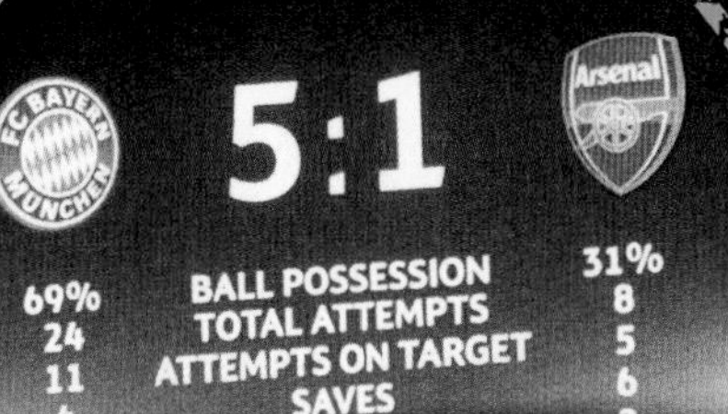

FC Bayern München	5:1	Arsenal
69%	BALL POSSESSION	31%
24	TOTAL ATTEMPTS	8
11	ATTEMPTS ON TARGET	5
4	SAVES	6
9	CORNERS	2
3	OFFSIDES	2
12	FOULS COMMITTED	11
2/0	YELLOW/RED CARDS	3/0

F = Fans
LIVERPOOL FC
YOU'LL NEVER WALK ALONE
The Premier League wouldn't be the same without them!
Introduced since the 2013-14 season, the Goal Decision System will never see a lawful goal be incorrectly ruled out.
G = Goal Decision System
H = Harry Kane
Can the England international win the Premier League Golden Boot for a third consecutive season?
When the Premier League takes a backseat and we are all left twiddling our thumbs. Weekends are never the same! What else are we supposed to do when our country is playing in San Marino?
I = International breaks
K = Kante
N'Golo Kante became just the second-ever player to win the Premier League title in successive seasons with different clubs (Leicester City and Chelsea). The midfielder was also crowned the PFA Players' Player of the Year in 2016-17.
J = Joker Jones
How will defending champions Chelsea fare without their legendary captain John Terry?
England defender Phil Jones is the best in the Premier League at pulling funny faces. More of the same please Phil!
L = Life without Terry?

M = Mourinho

Can Jose Mourinho help Manchester United claim their first Premier League title since 2013, when Sir Alex Ferguson's retired?

N = New Faces

Watch how summer signings, like Sead Kolasinac (Arsenal), Bernardo Silva (Manchester City) and Victor Lindelof (Manchester United), perform in their debut Premier League campaign...

O = Officials

We will forever scrutinise referees and their assistants, but there simply wouldn't be a game without them!

P = Promotion

Keep an eye out on the Championship table as well to see who wins promotion to the Premier League in 2018!

Q = Quest

The ultimate aim. Which team will lift the 2017-18 Premier League trophy? Can anyone stop Chelsea defending their title?

R = Relegation

Each season we wave goodbye to the bottom three teams, for whom the Championship awaits in 2018.

S = Selfies

T = Tattoos
The Premier League attracts some of the world's best players, as well as some of the most decorative stars. Check out Roberto Firmino's body ink!
No better example than Leicester City's remarkable triumph in 2015-16!
U = Underdogs
V = Venomous volleys
Like Emre Can's screamer at Watford last season!
The home of Tottenham Hotspur for the 2017-18 season.
W = Wembley Stadium
Lookout for a breakthrough of talented teenagers set to make their mark in the top-flight this campaign.
Y = Youngsters
The likes of Claudio Bravo (£17m), Lucas Perez (£17m) and Moussa Sissoko (£30m) slumped last season following their big money moves!
X = Xpensive Mistakes
The gruelling three-month wait between May and August for the next Premier League season...
Z = Zzzzzzz...

DID YOU KNOW?
Livermore had to wait 1,680 days to make his second appearance for England!

FACT FILE

NAME: Jake Cyril Livermore
POSITION: Midfielder
HEIGHT: 1.80m
DATE OF BIRTH: November 14, 1989
PLACE OF BIRTH: Enfield, London
CLUBS: Tottenham, Hull City, West Brom

JAKE LIVERMORE

Moving to West Bromwich Albion has worked wonders for Jake Livermore, as the midfielder relishes the challenge of helping England qualify for the 2018 FIFA World Cup finals next summer. The 27-year-old, who joined The Baggies back in January 2017 for £10 million, was recalled to The Three Lions squad after a near five-year absence following his impressive start to life at The Hawthorns.

A machine in England and West Brom's midfield engine room, *SHOOT* spoke exclusively to Livermore about his Midlands move, his thirst for classic cars and how he roared back onto the international stage.

WHO WAS IT THAT INTRODUCED YOU TO FOOTBALL?

It was actually my little cousin. I went to watch him play football once and his team were short of players, so I started playing for them. A Tottenham scout came to watch him a few weeks later, but they ended up signing both of us and it just excelled from there. I've always loved football, but I also used to box and enjoy cross country as a kid. My boxing and running fizzled out when I was about 16, my mum didn't want me to get hit anymore!

DO YOU HAVE A PRE-MATCH RITUAL?

Yeah, I'm a bit superstitious. I have to shower before a game, as soon as I get in the changing room. Then I always put everything on left first, whether it is left sock, shin pad or boot. It has always stuck since a kid.

YOU LEFT HULL CITY FOR WEST BROM EARLIER THIS YEAR. WHAT MADE YOU DECIDE TO JOIN THE BAGGIES?

I've always liked the manager [Tony Pulis]. He's brilliant, also a bit of a hothead, but that's only due to the fact he cares and believes in his system. He has always structured his players to know what they're doing on the field. Being a defensive midfielder, it's important for me to progress and know what I'm doing. He has given me an identity, a role that is niche.

YOU HAVE REPRESENTED YOUR COUNTRY, WON PROMOTION TO THE PREMIER LEAGUE AND PLAYED IN AN FA CUP FINAL. BUT, WHAT HAS BEEN THE BEST MOMENT OF YOUR CAREER, SO FAR?

It's probably putting on the England shirt the second time round. I think the first time, I was at Tottenham and I sort of grew into it. Whereas this time, it really meant something because I had been relegated, come back up through promotion [play-offs] and got my way back up the league again, making it much more special.

DID YOU KNOW?

Livermore says the best player he has ever played against is Chelsea legend Frank Lampard, who is also his footballing idol

YOU RETURNED TO THE ENGLAND SQUAD IN MARCH 2017 AND STARTED AGAINST GERMANY. DID YOU EXPECT THE RECALL?

No, it was a surprise! Pulis sent all of his staff to find me and bring me to his office. At that point, I was trying to avoid him. I had egged someone's car a couple of days before, so I thought I was in trouble! He sat me down, and to my surprise, he said he had received a call from The FA saying Gareth [Southgate] wanted me in his squad. That was one of the better moments.

HAVING MADE YOUR THREE LIONS DEBUT AGAINST ITALY BACK IN AUGUST 2012, OVER FIVE YEARS AGO, DID YOU EVER THINK YOUR INTERNATIONAL CAREER WAS OVER?

Yeah, of course I did. You're always hopeful and striving to get [back] there, but there was always that reality of thinking that the dream had sailed away. Thankfully I've worked hard and everything has been in the limelight for me to get that chance again.

LOOKING AHEAD TO THE 2018 FIFA WORLD CUP, GIVEN ENGLAND QUALIFY, WHAT DO YOU THINK YOU HAVE TO DO TO ENSURE YOU'RE INCLUDED IN SOUTHGATE'S SQUAD?

I can only put in on performances. I'm not going to be known for scoring goals, overly creating chances, going forward or being in and around the opposition's box. However, my job will be to have a role in the team which everyone is happy with. Hopefully if I carry on doing what my club want, then I will continue to be involved internationally as well.

AWAY FROM FOOTBALL, WE'VE ALSO HEARD YOU HAVE A LOVE FOR CLASSIC CARS...?

Yeah, I've always been very close to my dad. His passion when I was growing up was restoring classic cars, so when I was growing up, I would go down to the garage and help. Our relationship has stayed as strong as ever, so it's nice we still do it and I have got kids of my own now. We have probably restored over 20 cars together!

SPOT THE BALL

You know the drill! Here are four goalscoring opportunities from the 2016-17 season, but SHOOT has cheekily snatched the ball just before it hit the back of the net... Can you figure out which grid reference the ball was in for each strike?

1

Danny Welbeck (Arsenal) v Manchester United

2

Nathan Redmond (Southampton) v Watford

Henrikh Mkhitaryran (Manchester United) v Sunderland

Dele Alli (Tottenham) v Chelsea

CHECK YOUR ANSWERS ON PAGE 77!

10 THINGS YOU DIDN'T KNOW ABOUT...

PROFILE

HEIGHT: 1.88m
DATE OF BIRTH:
April 11, 1996
PLACE OF BIRTH:
Milton Keynes, England
NATIONAL TEAM:
England

Tottenham midfielder Dele Alli has taken the Premier League by storm since making his Spurs bow against Manchester United in August 2015. The England international, who starred for Milton Keynes Dons in League One prior to his switch to White Hart Lane, enjoyed a scintillating 2016-17 season, scoring 18 times for the North London outfit as they finished second to Premier League champions Chelsea. SHOOT has tipped Alli to go on and become a superstar for both club and country, but how much do you really know about the 21-year-old starlet? Here are 10 things you probably didn't know about the Spurs sensation...

Dele Alli

1. Alli passed his driving test first time, with just one minor fault.

2. His favourite TV show as a kid was 'Bananas in Pyjamas'.

3. Alli had several childhood heroes growing up, one of them being Jason Puncheon, with whom he played with at Milton Keynes Dons.

4. His first-ever touch in professional football was a back-heel for MK Dons in their 2012 FA Cup tie against Cambridge City.

5. Alli's first-ever game for Tottenham was a pre-season friendly... against Real Madrid!

6. As part of transfer negotiations, Liverpool set-up a meeting with Steven Gerrard for Alli in a bid to try and sign him from MK Dons. But, the Reds legend fell asleep!

7. In his first 50 Premier League games, Alli directly contributed to 26 goals (16 strikes and 10 assists), which is more than England legends Frank Lampard, Steven Gerrard and Paul Scholes.

8. Alli was eligible to represent Nigeria at international level due to his father, before making his senior England debut against France in November 2015.

9. He is a big fan of 'Five Guys', though he rarely eats that sort of food!

10. Alli is a Guinness World Record holder for the most figure of eight nutmegs in 30 seconds (8).

GOALKEEPER

DID YOU KNOW?

Cech started out as a midfielder during his youth career, until a leg break at the age of 10 saw him convert into a goalkeeper.

PETR CECH

CLUB: ARSENAL
HEIGHT: 1.96M
DATE OF BIRTH: May 20, 1982
PLACE OF BIRTH: PLZEN, CZECH REPUBLIC
NATIONAL TEAM: CZECH REPUBLIC

L	C	A	Z	M	A	W	S	O	N	G	J	W	V	W
A	S	X	X	Z	K	T	H	G	U	E	Y	E	X	K
L	E	H	F	U	Z	H	M	C	A	U	L	E	Y	Z
L	L	A	A	O	V	D	I	U	M	L	D	U	D	X
A	J	A	L	W	R	M	H	T	O	L	E	J	Z	R
N	K	W	S	D	C	S	X	E	A	B	T	K	L	K
A	C	A	A	C	E	R	T	V	A	R	B	S	I	N
L	M	L	J	R	E	R	O	E	A	T	Y	W	N	O
B	L	C	W	A	T	L	W	S	R	R	O	A	D	C
E	A	O	B	I	U	E	L	E	S	T	D	N	N	K
N	N	T	V	G	S	R	R	E	I	F	B	Y	U	A
T	Z	T	D	E	E	N	E	Y	S	R	R	R	Q	E
E	I	Z	A	Z	P	I	L	I	C	U	E	T	A	R
K	N	F	R	K	A	C	H	U	N	G	A	L	J	T
E	I	L	V	S	T	E	R	L	I	N	G	V	D	T

Hidden in this goal are 20 Premier League players. Your job is to find them all! Use the check list below to cross out the players you have already spotted.

- ARTER
- WALCOTT
- KNOCKAERT
- HEATON
- AZPILICUETA
- BENTEKE
- GUEYE
- KACHUNGA
- VARDY
- LALLANA
- STERLING
- MKHITARYAN
- LASCELLES
- FORSTER
- SHAWCROSS
- MAWSON
- ALDERWEIRELD
- DEENEY
- McAULEY
- LANZINI

Check your answers on page 77!

FACT FILE
NAME: Jill Louise Scott
POSITION: Midfielder
HEIGHT: 1.81m
DATE OF BIRTH:
February 2, 1987
PLACE OF BIRTH:
Sunderland, England
CLUBS: Sunderland,
Everton, Manchester City
DID YOU KNOW?
Scott used to be a highly-rated long-distance runner, winning the Mini London Marathon in 2000 and was North of England champion at 1500 metres at the age of 14
ENGLAND
MANCHESTER
18
94
CITY

Having grown up without any female football idols to look up to, Jill Scott has become one of the biggest names in women's football and is determined to inspire the next golden generation.

The 30-year-old midfielder, who has represented England over 120 times, is achieving unprecedented success with Manchester City Women after the Citizens claimed the 2016 FA Women's Super League 1 title, the 2017 FA Cup and the 2016 FA WSL Continental Cup recently.

Having starred for The Lionesses for over a decade, Scott spoke exclusively to *SHOOT* about being an Olympian, a champion and an inspiration as she launches her very own Football Academy Course.

DID YOU KNOW?

Scott's celebrity crush is former England captain David Beckham, who she met at Wimbledom in 2015

JILL SCOTT

WHEN DID YOU FIRST FALL IN LOVE WITH THE SPORT?

It was all I ever knew, playing football. I have been playing since I was six. I used to play with my Dad and brother and just had a real love for the game. I was probably the only girl in my school who wanted to play football. I joined my first team, an all-boys side, when I was about eight. I did used to get kicked and bullied a bit, but nothing was going to stop me playing.

AS A YOUNG ASPIRING GIRL, WHO DID YOU LOOK UP TO AND IDOLISE?

I supported Sunderland [men] and I went to all of the games with my granddad, he bought us a season ticket. I idolised the likes of Michael Gray, Kevin Phillips and Kevin Ball. It's mad because I have met all of them and I am a little bit in awe of them still. I told Kevin Ball that he was the reason I wanted to be a central midfielder because he was a proper hard case for Sunderland.

YOU ARE AMONG A SELECT FEW TO EARN OVER 100 INTERNATIONAL CAPS FOR ENGLAND. HOW DOES THAT RANK AMONG YOUR FOOTBALLING HONOURS?

It's definitely my proudest achievement. I was just so proud and I cannot believe it really, I still can't believe it now! It has been over 11 years since I made my England debut. It has just gone so quick!

YOU WERE ALSO PART OF THE GREAT BRITAIN TEAM TO COMPETE AT THE 2012 LONDON OLYMPIC GAMES. WHAT IS IT LIKE TO BE ABLE TO CALL YOURSELF AN OLYMPIAN?

It was just fantastic and I think we knew it could be a one-off experience. The Olympics is still my favourite tournament. I think tournaments are what makes you a better player.

DID YOU KNOW?
Scott is nicknamed "Crouchie" due to her height and performing a robot celebration after scoring a goal

THREE YEARS LATER, YOU WON A BRONZE MEDAL AT THE 2015 FIFA WORLD CUP FINALS IN CANADA, BEATING GERMANY IN THE PROCESS...

Yeah, it's crazy you are saying it is over two years ago! That is mad. To come back with a bronze medal, what a great achievement. It was such a journey. I think people only ever see what happens on the pitch, but everybody did their bit in order to get us that medal. I can't tell you anything that I'm meant to be doing this week, but if you tell us one moment in any tournament, I'll recite it! They are such fantastic memories and I'm looking forward to making more.

FOLLOWING THE LIONESSES' THIRD-PLACE HEROICS, THE WOMEN'S GAME EXPERIENCED A RISE IN ATTENDANCES AND PARTICIPATION. HAVE YOU BEEN IMPRESSED WITH THE REACTION SINCE ENGLAND'S WORLD CUP PERFORMANCE?

Yeah, it was great! When we are out on that pitch, we know that we are playing for the whole of women's football. So, we know if we do well, it means an extra game is going to be on the telly, meaning more people are going to be watching the game and then going to inspire another generation of young girls, and even young boys.

THE WOMEN'S SUPER LEAGUE SEASON IS RUNNING FROM SEPTEMBER TO MAY THIS TERM, ALONGSIDE THE MEN'S SCHEDULE. DO YOU THINK THIS IS A POSITIVE STEP FOR THE WOMEN'S GAME?

Yeah, I played in the league when it had this structure a few years ago when I was at Everton, I do welcome it. I think if they can sometimes double up the fixtures with people coming to the men's and women's games, that has worked well for us in the past. There are always pros and cons. But the way the clubs are running it now, it is very professional and the attendances are getting better all the time.

LAST YEAR, THE CLUB WON THE WOMEN'S SUPER LEAGUE 1 TITLE, THE FA CUP AND THE CONTINENTAL CUP. WHAT IS THE NEXT BIG AIM FOR MANCHESTER CITY?

We do definitely need to start looking at the Champions League. But at the same time, last year it was our debut season in it. To reach a semi-final, I don't think we really looked at that achievement as much as we should have. It's just about getting that consistency now in that tournament. Hopefully this year we'll set the benchmark even higher in that competition.

ON A PERSONAL NOTE, YOU'RE EXCITINGLY LAUNCHING YOUR VERY OWN JILL SCOTT FOOTBALL ACADEMY COURSE. IT'S BEING SET-UP TO TRY AND COUNTERACT AGAINST THE DROP-OFF IN FEMALE PARTICIPATION FROM THE AGE OF 16. WHERE DID THIS IDEA COME FROM?

Soccer Camps are something that I have been doing for a few years now around the UK. I love it. The reason that I'm keeping it girls only at the minute is because when I used to go out, I was the only girl and there used to be like 30 boys. I think since having just girls, there have been a few who have said their confidence is so much better now, rather than having that experience at a boys' team. People will probably class it as work, coaching 30 to 40 kids, but I join in and have a good day. I attended an academy when I was 16, up until I was 18, up in Gateshead, and without that, I don't think I would have been selected to play for England. It was an opportunity to play football three, four times a week and get support in terms of your training. So when this opportunity came up, I couldn't really say no! I really like to improve players.

YOU WILL BE PERSONALLY COACHING THOSE ASPIRING GIRLS EACH WEEK. IS TURNING YOUR HAND TO MANAGEMENT SOMETHING YOU ARE CONSIDERING IN THE PROFESSIONAL GAME?

Yeah, I think that is what I will want to do. Everyone keeps talking about this transition period, so I'm either starting to get rubbish or getting old, but you do have to start thinking about that next bit because it will be such a shock when you stop playing the game. I can't really imagine leaving the game, so if an opportunity came where I could coach, that would be fantastic. Everyone goes on about the facilities here at Manchester City, but I'm just more intrigued by all the knowledge. I love just walking round and speaking to people and learning every day from such great professionals.

WHAT ABOUT POTENTIALLY STEPPING UP YOUR MEDIA PORTFOLIO?

I think I have got a face for radio! I think it's great that women footballers' opinions are being appreciated because I think that at the end of the day, it is just gender. We have played the game for as long as the men, some of them even longer. Our knowledge is of a high standard. It's not like we come train and then go home and do our nails, we are constantly watching football and we just have a love for the game. I have done a few little bits like co-commentary, and I do like to talk, so who knows!

WHAT TIPS DO YOU HAVE FOR ANY *SHOOT* READERS WANTING TO BECOME THE NEXT JILL SCOTT?

Just keep making the right decisions. I never really set myself massive long-term goals because I always believe that if you make the right decisions every day, and work as hard as you can, then the rest will fall into place. So I would say keep on enjoying it, especially at a young age, because there are some days where it's like football overload. I always tell the kids that it's not about training every single day, pushing yourself as much as you can every day, I think you do need to have that mental break and switch off. Get a good balance. Just enjoy it, work hard and do it with a smile on your face as well.

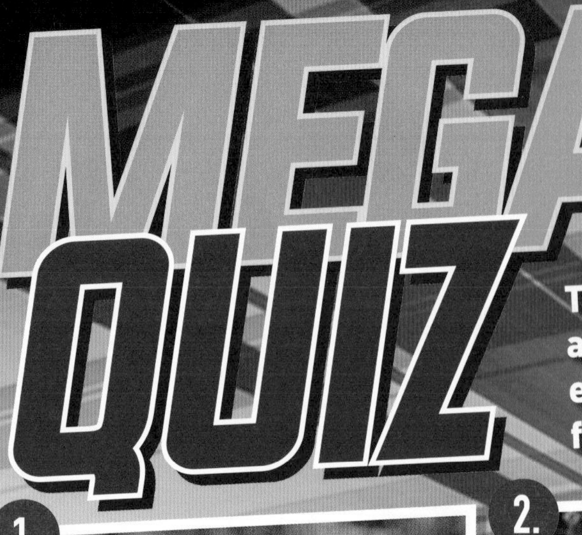

MEGA QUIZ

FIRST-HALF

Think you know your football? Come and have a go if you think you're smart enough! Test your knowledge with the first-half of *SHOOT's* bumper footy quiz...

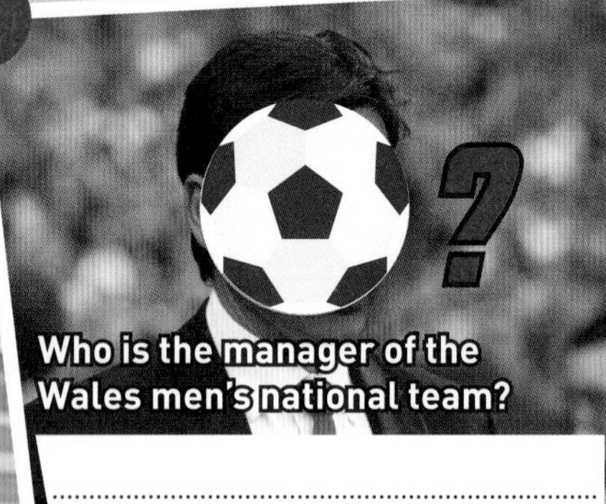

1. Who is the manager of the Wales men's national team?

2. Which player scored the winning goal in the 2017 FA Cup final?

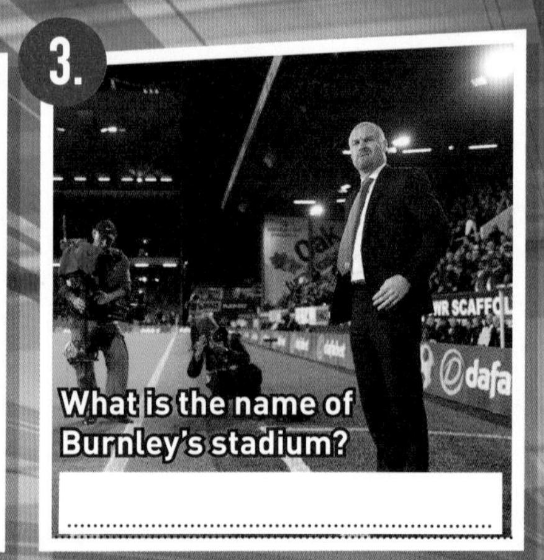

3. What is the name of Burnley's stadium?

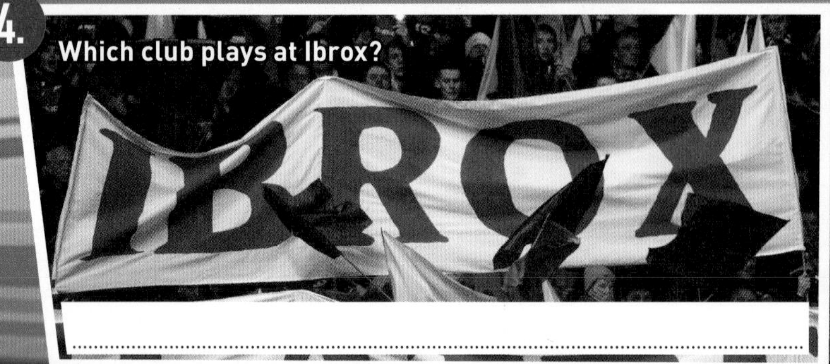

4. Which club plays at Ibrox?

5. Which player won the 2016-17 Premier League Golden Boot?

6. In 2017, Newcastle United, Brighton and Hove Albion and which other club won promotion to the Premier League?

7. Which player won the 2017 PFA Player of the Year award?

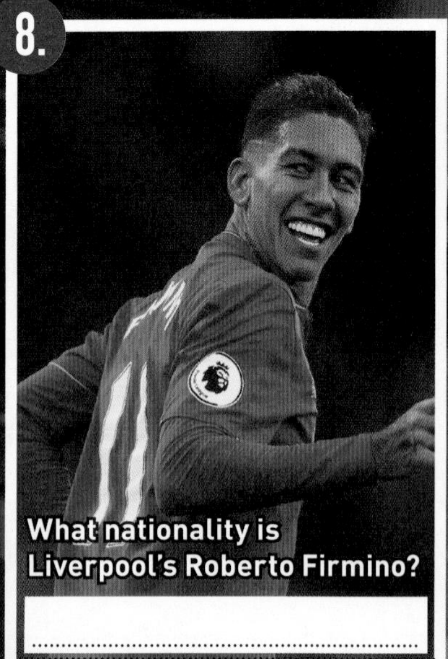

8. What nationality is Liverpool's Roberto Firmino?

9.

Manchester United defeated which club to lift the 2017 UEFA Europa League?

....

10.

What was the score between Juventus and Real Madrid in the 2017 UEFA Champions League Final?

....

11.

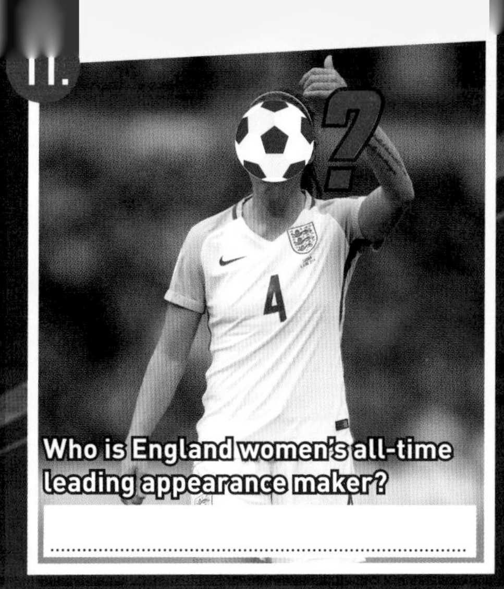

Who is England women's all-time leading appearance maker?

....

12.

Since 1992, who has won more Premier League titles - Arsenal or Manchester City?

....

13.

Which country will host the 2018 FIFA World Cup?

....

14.

From which club did Chelsea sign Pedro from?

....

15.

Fernandinho, Miguel Britos and which other player received two red cards during the 2016-17 Premier League season?

....

16.

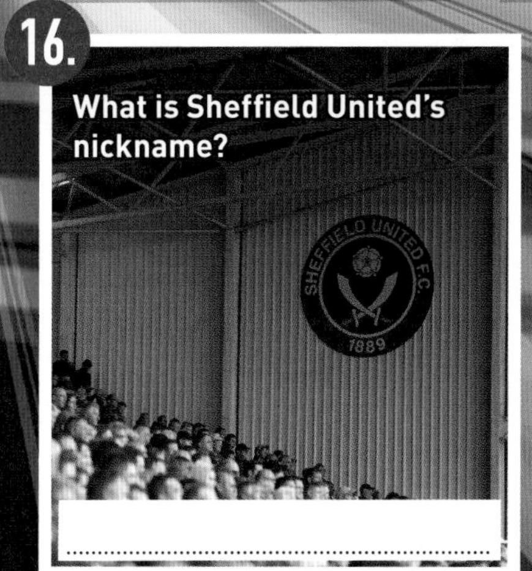

What is Sheffield United's nickname?

....

17.

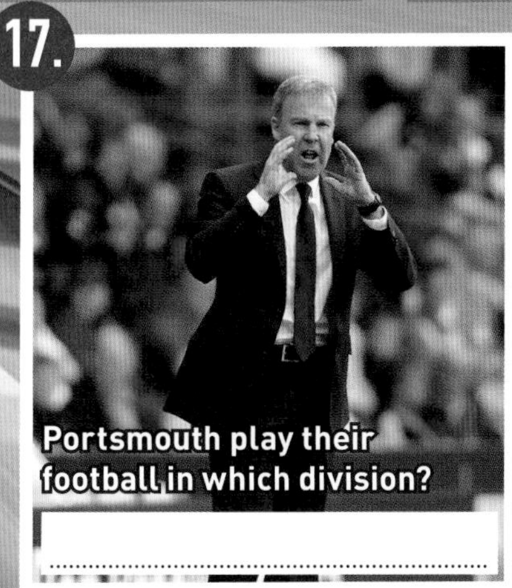

Portsmouth play their football in which division?

....

18.

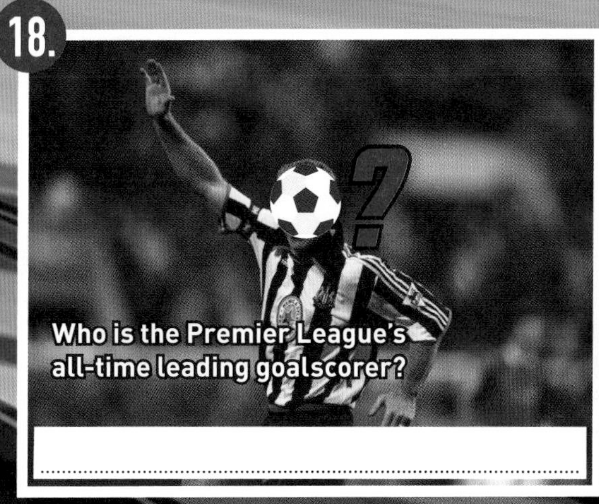

Who is the Premier League's all-time leading goalscorer?

....

19.

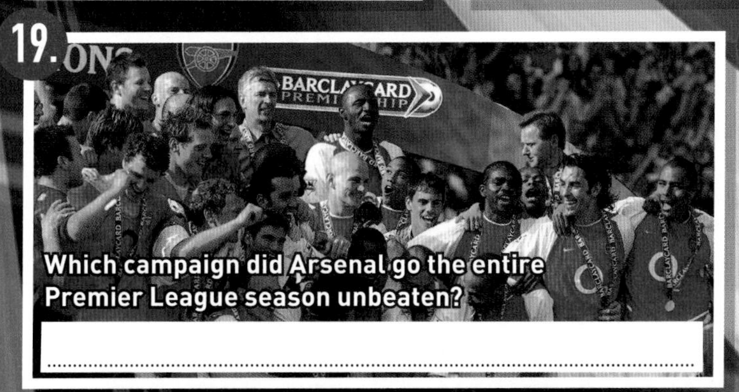

Which campaign did Arsenal go the entire Premier League season unbeaten?

....

20.

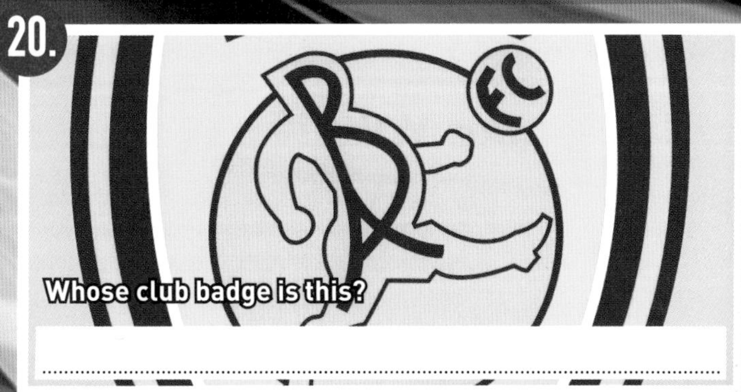

Whose club badge is this?

....

There goes the half-time whistle! Grab a drink, take a breather and head to page 60 for the second-half of *SHOOT's* Mega Quiz...

SHOOT FOR THE STARS

In the last few seasons, we have seen the likes of Marcus Rashford and Dele Alli undertake meteoric rises from the depths of the unknown to the forefront of world football. The 2017-18 campaign will present a whole new crop of talented starlets from the Premier League 2 or Under-18 sides that golden opportunity to break into the first-team picture. *SHOOT* has highlighted ten youngsters in English football who could be catching your eye this season.

"I grew up reading SHOOT, so it's an absolute privilege to actually feature in it!"

FACT FILE

POSITION: Defender
DATE OF BIRTH: December 24, 1999
NATIONALITY: English
CLUB: Aston Villa

TOP TARGET FOR 2017-18:
"I would like to make a few first-team appearances. I need to build up my strength and become more vocal as a centre-back – it is an important part of my game."

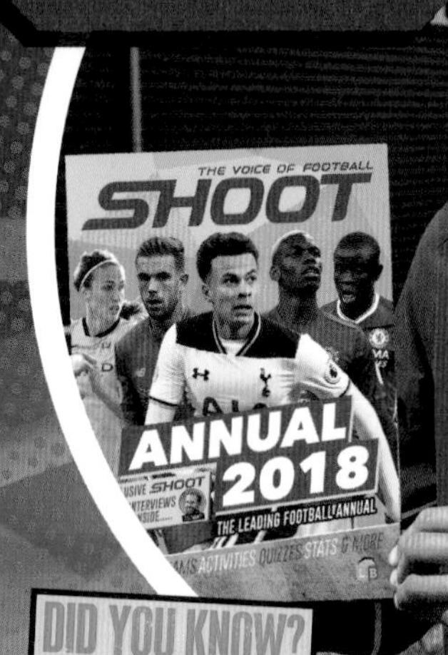

Jacob Bedeau

Aston Villa defender Bedeau has already had a taste of league football after playing seven times for Bury prior to moving to Villa Park in January 2017. The 17-year-old clearly impressed the Villa hierarchy to spend almost a £1,000,000 on the youngster's services, and his fine performances for their Under-23 side in the second-half of the 2016-17 season further underlined his potential. Bedeau made six appearances for The Villans to help them finish seventh in the Premier League 2, and he trained with Steve Bruce's first-team in March as he nears a senior debut for the Championship outfit. Having been targeted by some of England's biggest clubs prior to signing for Villa, Bedeau clearly has the potential for a bright future in the game.

DID YOU KNOW?
The defender was watched by 27 scouts during his final appearances for Bury and attracted interest from the likes of Manchester United, Manchester City and Liverpool

FACT FILE

POSITION: Defender
DATE OF BIRTH: March 17, 2000
NATIONALITY: English
CLUB: Southampton

Jake Vokins

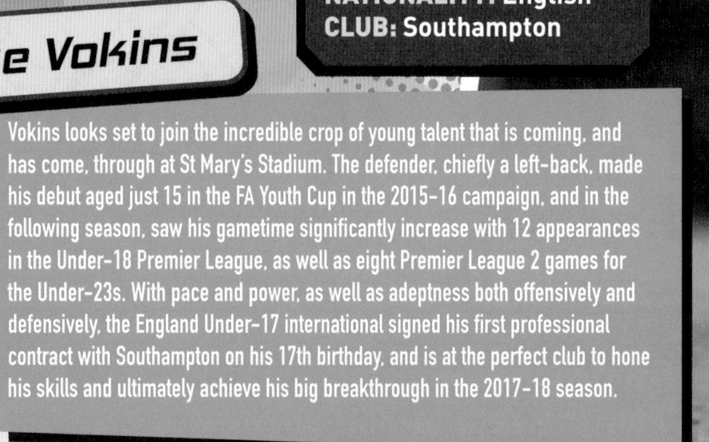

Vokins looks set to join the incredible crop of young talent that is coming, and has come, through at St Mary's Stadium. The defender, chiefly a left-back, made his debut aged just 15 in the FA Youth Cup in the 2015-16 campaign, and in the following season, saw his gametime significantly increase with 12 appearances in the Under-18 Premier League, as well as eight Premier League 2 games for the Under-23s. With pace and power, as well as adeptness both offensively and defensively, the England Under-17 international signed his first professional contract with Southampton on his 17th birthday, and is at the perfect club to hone his skills and ultimately achieve his big breakthrough in the 2017-18 season.

Trevoh Chalobah

FACT FILE

POSITION: Defender
DATE OF BIRTH: July 5, 1999
NATIONALITY: English
CLUB: Chelsea

Part of the FA Youth Cup winning sides of 2016 and 2017, 18-year-old Chalobah is a highly-rated defender set for a bright future in the game. The England youth international signed for the West London outfit at the tender age of nine, before making his Under-18 debut for The Blues just five years later, a season which saw him play in every position across the backline. He soon became a major figure on the youth scene after captaining the Under-18s in the 2014-15 campaign, before going onto appear for the Under-23 side on a regular basis in the succeeding seasons. Chalobah has also captained his country at a major tournament, leading the Under-17 team at the 2016 UEFA European Championships. Following the departure of the legendary John Terry at Stamford Bridge, the fellow centre-half may well earn his senior Chelsea debut in the 2017-18 season.

Morgan Feeney

Having already trained with the first-team and battled the likes of Romelu Lukaku, centre-half Feeney will be hoping that the 2017-18 campaign sees him make his Everton senior debut. Given his efforts over recent years, he won't be far away, with the 18-year-old defender having already made the step-up to Under-23 level, appearing 11 times for the title-winning Toffees side in the Premier League 2 last term. Part of an Everton backline that conceded just 21 goals in 2016-17, Feeney has also had success when called upon at international level, with the starlet playing in all four of England's games at the Under-17 UEFA European Championships in 2016. He has since become an integral part of the Young Lions camp after captaining the Under-18s on numerous occasions last season.

FACT FILE

POSITION: Defender
DATE OF BIRTH: February 8, 1999
NATIONALITY: English
CLUB: Everton

Max Bird

FACT FILE

POSITION: Midfielder
DATE OF BIRTH: September 18, 2000
NATIONALITY: English
CLUB: Derby County

Derby's versatile midfielder Bird is already making great strides at the tender age of just 16. The Rams gem scored a 25-yard free-kick for the Under-16 side to help them win the Blades Cup back in October 2016, beating Manchester United in a penalty shootout. Since then, he has made 18 appearances in the Under-18 Premier League, scoring four times, including twice against West Brom. The teenager has also seen his meteoric rise take another huge step in 2017 by appearing nine times for the Under-23 team in the Premier League 2, helping them to an eighth place finish. Bird can also play in defence to further underline his credentials ahead of what looks a very promising career.

Angel Gomes

When it comes to goalscoring midfielders in the youth ranks, there aren't many better than Manchester United's Gomes. The England Under-17 international made his Under-18 debut for The Red Devils aged just 15 and immediately became a key cog in their midfield in the 2015-16 season, before adding goals to his game the following campaign. Gomes scored 12 goals in just 20 games for the Under-18s as United finished second behind neighbours City in the U18 Premier League. The gifted Gomes then fulfilled his dream towards the end of the 2016-17 term by appearing in Jose Mourinho's first-team on the final day of the Premier League season, replacing captain Wayne Rooney for the final few minutes in their win over Crystal Palace. He is also already making headway on the international scene, and will certainly take confidence from Marcus Rashford's incredible rise to fame over the last couple of years as he looks to add to his senior Red Devils debut in the 2017-18 campaign.

FACT FILE

POSITION: Midfielder
DATE OF BIRTH: August 31, 2000
NATIONALITY: English
CLUB: Manchester United

Samuel Shashoua

FACT FILE

POSITION: Midfielder
DATE OF BIRTH: May 13, 1999
NATIONALITY: English
CLUB: Tottenham Hotspur

Attacking midfielder Shashoua began his scholarship at Tottenham in the summer of 2015, and is slowly but surely making his way up through the youth ranks. The 18-year-old made his Under-18 debut back in the 2014-15 season, before going onto make 18 appearances and net four goals in the succeeding campaign as Spurs finished eighth in the League 1 South Division. Last term also saw Shashoua make great strides, scoring a sensational 13 goals in 23 games for Tottenham as they replicated their seventh place finish, and the youngster also earned four starts in the Premier League 2 for the Under-23 outfit. With a goal and an assist in the UEFA Youth League in 2016, as well as a substitute spot for the senior team in their 6-1 thrashing of Leicester City back in May, Shashoua's senior Spurs bow could be on the horizon.

Liam Cullen

FACT FILE

POSITION: Striker
DATE OF BIRTH: April 23, 1999
NATIONALITY: Welsh
CLUB: Swansea City

There aren't many players in the Under-18 Premier League who have scored more goals than Swansea's Cullen last season. The 18-year-old forward bagged 16 strikes in just 21 appearances, and with The Swans netting just 34 times in the division, the Wales youth international is clearly the star man and the one they look to for goals. His excellent goalscoring form at youth level has seen him play twice at Under-23 level in the Premier League 2, and in just his second match, Cullen netted a brilliant brace in a 4-1 win at Stoke City back in April. He has been at the Liberty Stadium since the age of eight, and given that he has occasionally trained with the first-team already, Cullen could soon be called up to the senior side heading into the 2017-18 season.

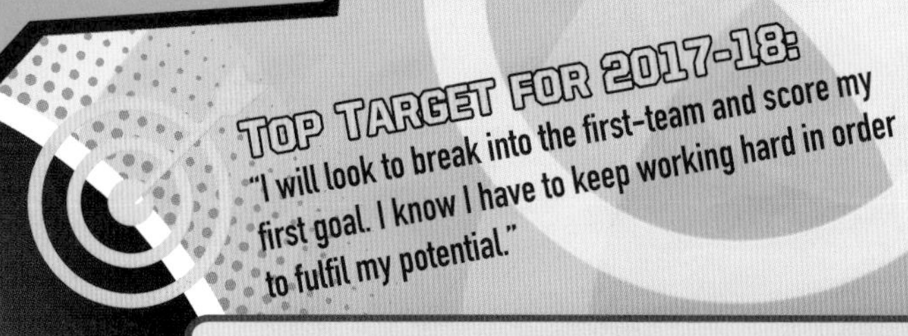

"It's an honour to be included in this year's SHOOT Annual, especially among all these great young talents."

TOP TARGET FOR 2017-18:
"I will look to break into the first-team and score my first goal. I know I have to keep working hard in order to fulfil my potential."

FACT FILE
POSITION: Striker
DATE OF BIRTH: August 28, 2000
NATIONALITY: English
CLUB: Reading

Danny Namaso Loader

Reading striker Loader has proven to many this season exactly why he has the potential to play at the top level. The 17-year-old was in good goalscoring form during the 2016-17 season, scoring a total of 12 goals in 33 appearances for club and country, including a brace against Tottenham Hotspur. With six appearances in Premier League 2 as well, Loader is making his way through the ranks at The Royals. International caps at Under-16 and Under-17 level with England, as well as goals to match, he looks set to make his senior Reading debut in the near future.

DID YOU KNOW?
Loader's elder brother, Ben, is an England Under-19 international rugby union player

"Just want to say thanks to SHOOT for the recognition, much appreciated!"

TOP TARGET FOR 2017-18:
"To make my Premier League debut. Hopefully if I work hard, then I'll get my chance"

DID YOU KNOW?
Tyrese is the son of former Arsenal and Everton striker Kevin Campbell, who made 325 Premier League appearances during his career, netting 82 goals

Tyrese Campbell

Stoke City forward Campbell seems to score goals whatever level he plays at. The 17-year-old, who joined The Potters from Manchester City in October 2016, scored six goals in just eight games in last season's Under-18 Premier League, which helped Stoke finish eighth in the North Division. However, it was in the Premier League 2 where he really made his name, with the England Under-17 international netting three times in just 11 appearances, including both goals in a 2-0 victory over Aston Villa. With Campbell becoming an increasingly prominent member of the Under-23 side at the bet365 Stadium, the backroom staff clearly rate him highly, so don't be too surprised to see him turning out for the senior team in the 2017-18 campaign.

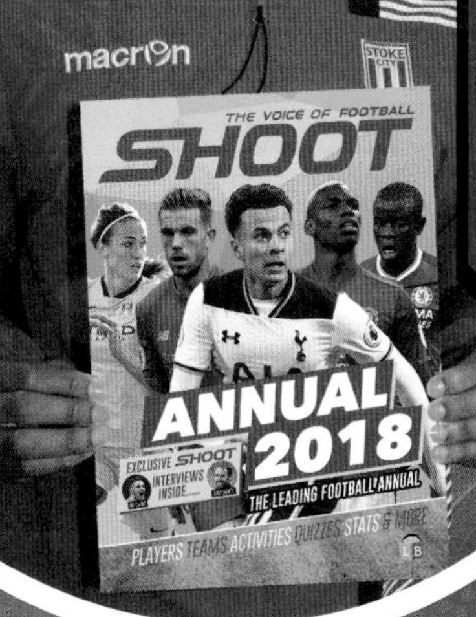

FACT FILE
POSITION: Striker
DATE OF BIRTH: December 28, 1999
NATIONALITY: English
CLUB: Stoke City

Jack Butland

DID YOU KNOW?
Butland's icon is Italy's legendary shot stopper Gianluigi Buffon

Having recovered from the "worst moment of his career", Jack Butland is back fighting fit and playing at the top of his game in a bid to become England's number one goalkeeper ahead of the 2018 FIFA World Cup.

The 24-year-old was restricted to just five Premier League appearances for Stoke City last season after fracturing his ankle against Germany back in March 2016 – a horrendous injury that ultimately sidelined the shot stopper for almost 13 months.

But with next summer's major tournament just around the corner, the Bristol-born star is now relishing the battle against the likes of Joe Hart, Fraser Forster, Tom Heaton and Jordan Pickford to claim the Three Lions' No.1 jersey in Russia.

SHOOT spoke exclusively to Butland about his upbringing, England euphoria, World Cup dream and his top tips for you aspiring goalkeepers out there!

FACT FILE

NAME: Jack Butland
POSITION: Goalkeeper
HEIGHT: 1.96m
DATE OF BIRTH: March 10, 1993
PLACE OF BIRTH: Bristol, England
CLUBS: Birmingham City, Cheltenham Town (loan), Stoke City, Barnsley (loan), Leeds United (loan), Derby County (loan)

FIRST OF ALL, WHERE DID YOUR FOOTBALLING CAREER ALL BEGIN?

"Growing up, both my dad and granddad played rugby, we were a very sporty family. But I joined Clevedon United and was there until I was about 15-years-old. That was my first taste of football. I was a striker until I was about 12! Then our goalkeeper got injured one day. We were getting hammered as someone else went in goal. He soon had enough. So I said I will have a go, and it just seemed to stick. But I do miss playing up front!"

AS WELL AS BEING A PROMISING FOOTBALLER, WEREN'T YOU A TALENTED RUGBY PLAYER TOO?

"Yeah, around the time I had a football trial with Birmingham City, when I was about 13 or 14, I was also part of a select few from my school that were put forward for a rugby open day. Then all of a sudden I signed for Birmingham and they said you're going to have to quit rugby because we don't want you getting injured. My friends and ex-coaches said I could have had a really good shot at rugby."

IS IT ALSO TRUE THAT YOU ONCE GOT THE BETTER OF ENGLAND RUGBY UNION INTERNATIONAL BILLY VUNIPOLA?

"It is! He used to play for Castle School and we got to the final of the Year 8 Somerset Schools Cup. Our team quickly got word that they had this big, big kid playing for them, so we thought "Oh no!". He was their focal point and we just tried to tackle him in twos and threes. My favourite moment was when he broke through the middle. I was quicker than him, so I managed to tap tackle him. I remember he hit the floor in disgust, turned round and threw the ball at me! He had a proper strop. I got the better of him then and we won the final. That was the talk of the school for a while."

WHAT SOME PEOPLE MAY NOT KNOW ABOUT YOU IS THE FACT YOU ARE AN OLYMPIAN. WHAT WAS IT LIKE COMPETING AT THE 2012 LONDON GAMES?

"It was surreal and a completely different world. You saw the likes of Usain Bolt, LeBron James and [Sir] Chris Hoy, it was amazing to see them. Personally I was starstruck. It was incredible to see how other sports do things and their professionalism, because they are on a four-year cycle to have one shot to be the best in the world. It would have been nice to have a medal to go with it, but it was certainly an experience that me and my family will never forget."

SHORTLY AFTER THE OLYMPICS, YOU BECAME ENGLAND'S YOUNGEST EVER GOALKEEPER AFTER MAKING YOUR DEBUT AGAINST ITALY. WHAT CAN YOU RECALL FROM THAT SPECIAL MOMENT?

"I knew I was in the squad, as Joe Hart was injured. We took two goalkeepers, me and John Ruddy. The goalie coach, David Watson, who I worked with at Birmingham, pulled me aside during the training camp and said, "Are you ready?". No! I didn't tell him that, but of course I wasn't. You can never be ready to make your England debut. It was when Roy Hodgson announced the teamsheet before the game that I saw it for real. My heart just sank and everything just came over me. I was about to play for England! I don't remember a single thing from the game. I only remember what happened because of the highlights. After the game, I went up and saw my parents, they were in tears and I was pretty much crying. It took days, weeks even, to settle down and stop thinking about it."

HOW MUCH WOULD IT MEAN TO YOU TO BECOME ENGLAND'S NUMBER ONE GOALKEEPER?

"It is the ultimate thing in football, to represent your country. You see how passionate I am. I hate it when people say we're not good enough. It's not that we're not good enough, it's just that we are not showing it, especially at major tournaments. It hurts me because I want to be a part of something special. I want England to be back on top. I dream about winning a World Cup, dream about being part of a team that shuts everyone up and proves that we can be the best team in the world. People will laugh at us, but that is what we all believe we can do."

HAS THE APPOINTMENT OF MANAGER GARETH SOUTHGATE INSTILLED THIS CONFIDENCE AND OPTIMISM WITHIN THE ENGLAND SQUAD?

"Yeah, I am excited, and I do think it is down to Gareth to be honest. It has taken someone, like the manager, to take a risk and put their body on the line and say we can't keep doing what we have done before. He has given everyone a wake-up call, a shock to the system. The first thing he did when he came in was to be completely honest on why he took the job. He wants to make a difference and he believes that he can. When your manager comes in and believes in himself like that, it's really difficult for you not to think the same. He has been through the highest of the highs and the lowest of the lows as a player himself, so the squad can compare themselves to him. I think that was the biggest thing in starting this journey. He is prepared to visit really hard and dark times, be open about it and we are now seeing players standing up, being open, being honest and getting better. I believe we can do something special."

LOOKING AHEAD TO RUSSIA, WHO WOULD YOU SAY ARE ENGLAND'S THREE KEY MEN?

"I'll start with Dele Alli. As a talent, he is young, hungry and extremely skillful. He has got that flash and flair that we are used to seeing from the Brazilians or Spanish. He is our little Brazilian if you like. He has got that edge about him, where he can unlock any team and he is just extremely special. Then you have got Marcus Rashford, someone who has come out of nowhere for Manchester United and just grabbed the game by the scruff of the neck. He has scored massive goals for United and shown fearlessness. He is young, quick, skillful, can score goals and he is just exciting to watch. And then there's Harry Kane. People wrote him off after the first year [he broke through], saying he wasn't going to do it again. But he has done it again and again, winning another Golden Boot. He is a top goalscorer and I think in the next couple of years, and hopefully in next year's World Cup, he is going to establish himself as one of the best strikers in the world."

DID YOU KNOW?

One of Butland's favourite hobbies is clay pigeon shooting

WHAT ABOUT YOURSELF PERSONALLY, HAVING ESTABLISHED YOURSELF AT CLUB AND COUNTRY LEVEL, WHAT IS YOUR NEXT ULTIMATE AIM IN FOOTBALL?

"My focus has always been to be the best I can be, but I don't want to finish my career without winning things. Most importantly, I want to be successful with England. I also want to be playing Champions League football and competing for titles and cups. Ultimately I want to finish next summer with a winner's medal. That is the goal."

TO ACHIEVE THAT, DO YOU FEEL YOU HAVE TO BE PLAYING FOR ONE OF THE 'TOP CLUBS'?

"Yeah, I'm not going to beat around the bush or lie about it, but I want to play at the top level. I stand by why I joined Stoke City at the time, I didn't want to go to a top club and just be another number. I wanted to earn my place. Ultimately, the end goal is to go again. I don't just want to be involved in the Premier League or cups, I want to win cups. I don't just want to be in an England squad, I want to be winning stuff with England. I am proud that I have done as well as I have, but I want something to show for it and something to be proud of."

HAVING GROWN UP SUPPORTING MANCHESTER UNITED, WOULD THAT BE YOUR DREAM MOVE?

"Yeah. From a sentimental value, I think United is the pinnacle, or would be the choice if I had the option. If everything fell into place and it was Manchester United, if you told me that as an eight or nine-year-old, I think that would be the dream."

WHAT ARE YOUR TOP THREE TIPS FOR ANY *SHOOT* READERS WHO WANT TO BE THE NEXT JACK BUTLAND?

1. "You have got to believe and got to be resilient. I think as a kid, when you are growing up, you can never give up. The moment you give up, all of those opportunities and all of that potential is gone.

2. "Make the most of the opportunities you are given. If you are passionate about football, don't cut any corners, do whatever it is you can do to make it. Do that extra practice out in the rain, get yourself to the gym, all of those little things that you can do to be better.

3. "Study. Look at the best, look what they do, look at people in your position and pick out positives and negatives. Try and be the best, then you can have no regrets at the end of it."

JOHN STONES

CLUB:
MANCHESTER CITY
HEIGHT: 1.88M
DATE OF BIRTH:
May 28, 1994
PLACE OF BIRTH:
BARNSLEY, ENGLAND
NATIONAL TEAM:
ENGLAND

DID YOU KNOW?

Stones became the most expensive defender in Premier League history after joining Manchester City from Everton in a deal worth an initial £47.5 million.

FUNNY FACES

A

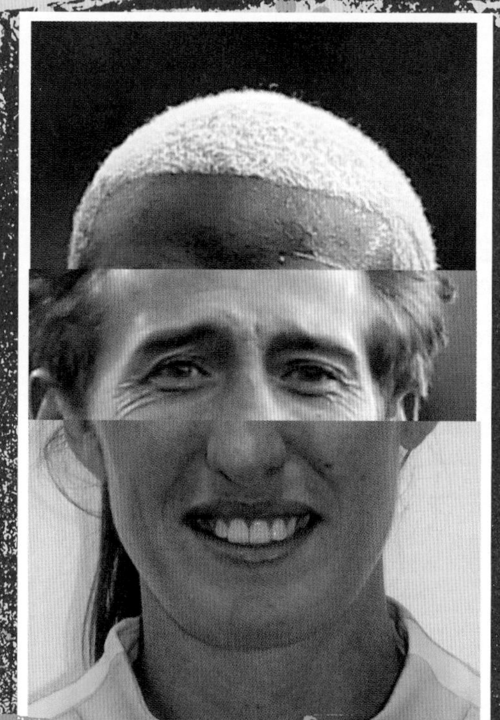

SHOOT have got these famous male and female footballers' faces all mixed up! Can you recognise who is who from their hair, eyes and mouth?

CHECK YOUR ANSWERS ON PAGE 77!

B

C

A

HAIR:

EYES:

MOUTH:

B

HAIR:

EYES:

MOUTH:

C

HAIR:

EYES:

MOUTH:

Route to RUSS

The 2018 FIFA World Cup is almost upon us, with the major tournament being hosted in Russia for the first time in the competition's history, as 32 countries battle it out for the world's ultimate footballing prize. But will anybody be able to stop Germany reclaiming their crown?

England, Wales, Scotland, Republic of Ireland and Northern Ireland are all fighting for a top two finish in their respective qualifying groups, though only the group winner automatically qualifies for the finals, with each second placed side being ranked among the other runners-up to determine the play-off contenders.

Here is *SHOOT's* fun fact file on each country ahead of this summer's finals.

Harry Kane

England

Nickname: The Three Lions
Stadium: Wembley Stadium
Highest FIFA Ranking: 3rd (August 2012)
Key Man: Harry Kane
The Boss: Gareth Southgate

Best World Cup Finals Result: Winners (1966)
All-Time Goalscorer: Wayne Rooney (53)
All-Time Appearance Maker: Peter Shilton (125 caps)

Gareth Southgate

Robbie Brady

Republic of Ireland

Nickname: The Boys in Green
Stadium: Aviva Stadium
Highest FIFA Ranking: 6th (August 1993)
Key Man: Robbie Brady
The Boss: Martin O'Neill

Best World Cup Finals Result: Quarter-Finals (1990)
All-Time Goalscorer: Robbie Keane (68)
All-Time Appearance Maker: Robbie Keane (146 caps)

Martin O'Neill

Gareth Bale
Nickname: The Dragons
Stadium: Cardiff City Stadium
Highest FIFA Ranking: 8th (October 2015)
Key Man: Gareth Bale
The Boss: Chris Coleman
Wales
Best World Cup Finals Result:
Quarter-Finals (1958)
All-Time Goalscorer: Ian Rush (28)
All-Time Appearance Maker:
Neville Southall (92 caps)
Chris Coleman
Steven Davis
Nickname: Green and White Army
Stadium: Windsor Park
Highest FIFA Ranking: 25th (June 2016)
Key Man: Steven Davis
The Boss: Michael O'Neill
Northern Ireland
Best World Cup Finals Result:
Quarter-Finals (1958)
All-Time Goalscorer: David Healy (36)
All-Time Appearance Maker:
Pat Jennings (119 caps)
Michael O'Neill
Robert Snodgrass
Nickname: The Tartan Army
Stadium: Hampden Park
Highest FIFA Ranking: 13th (October 2007)
Key Man: Robert Snodgrass
The Boss: Gordon Strachan
Scotland
Best World Cup Finals Result:
Group Stages (1954, 1958, 1974, 1978, 1982, 1986, 1990, 1998)
All-Time Goalscorer: Kenny Dalglish and Denis Law (30)
All-Time Appearance Maker:
Kenny Dalglish (102 caps)
Gordon Strachan

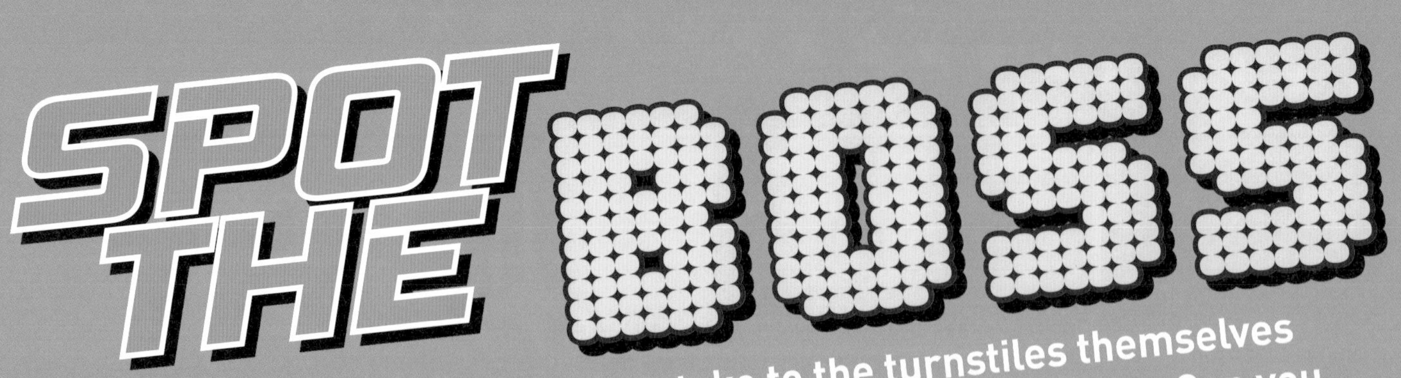

On a rare day off, managers love to take to the turnstiles themselves and hide among football fans to secretly scout the opposition. Can you spot all 10 bosses in this crowd?

Mauricio Pochettino

Tony Pulis Chris Hughton Brendan Rodgers

Antonio Conte David Wagner Eddie Howe

Pep Guardiola Sean Dyche Jurgen Klopp

Despite failing to win a major honour since lifting the 1966 FIFA World Cup, Gareth Southgate is determined for England to become the best in the world again. The 47-year-old succeeded Sam Allardyce as Three Lions manager in November 2016 following an impressive three-year reign as England Under-21 boss. Former defender Southgate, who earned 57 international caps for England between 1995 and 2004, spoke exclusively to *SHOOT* about his transition from man-marker to manager, his ultimate goal as Three Lions boss and his top tips for those of you who dream of playing for your country!

GARETH SOUTHGATE

Congratulations on the England job Gareth! What was it like being appointed manager of your country?

It's a great opportunity. I'm hugely proud to be in a position like this, which brings great responsibility, but it's about being successful. I'm proud of the international caps that I got, but we didn't win anything. We got closer than anybody else over the last 30 years, but ultimately you want to win trophies and that is the same if you are a player or a coach. My job is to try to progress the team and help the squad improve. They're young and not where they want to be yet, so there is a lot of potential in there.

Becoming national team boss, is that the highlight of your entire footballing career?

Making my England debut was a dream I had for 20 years. As soon as I started to kick a ball, my one thing was to play for England. So that, because of how long it took and the steps I had to go through to get there, was in my mind really difficult and a long process. Equally, if you are going to manage, you want to manage big clubs and the national team, so I'm very proud to do that. But the pathway to management has been a little different, so I guess I wouldn't dismiss my first England cap and playing in a tournament at home [UEFA Euro 96] as being my proudest moments.

As a former international player, now national team manager, what have you discovered are the main differences between each role?

Sleep! I used to sleep nearly all day, and now I hardly sleep at all. I would say as manager, it's responsibility. You're responsible for everybody and everything. As a player, you feel responsibility, but in actual fact, your focus is mainly on yourself, your performance, your training and your preparation. The breadth of what you do as a player is narrower. As a manager, you are trying to think of every way to improve everybody within the team, including the staff and players.

Which is more nerve-racking, playing for England or managing your country?

I think playing is actually still one of the hardest things because every player, before they step out, has that anxiety of how am I going to be today? For the manager, your work is predominantly done during the week. You can affect things during the game with changes and communication, but most of your work is done. I wouldn't underestimate how difficult it's to play and pull the boots on and go out there every week and deliver. I think both have different challenges, but both are challenging.

You spent three years as England Under-21 boss, was that tenure the ideal stepping stone ahead of the senior managerial role for you?

I think it's great preparation for the role because most of the challenges you face are the same. The difference is the spotlight and intensity around the matches, it's that simple. There's a lot more media focus on our performances, results and everything else that goes on around the camp. But in terms of the day-to-day challenges and the job itself, you are dealing with slightly older players, so I think that needs a slightly different approach. I think it's important to bear in mind their experiences and their seniority. They are men, so you treat them slightly differently. Not that I treated the Under-21s as young kids, they are also maturing into men, but their understanding of tactical concepts or technical things sometimes isn't as far developed as some of the older ones.

Following Roy Hodgson's resignation after Euro 2016, you didn't want the England job. What changed after Sam Allardyce's short spell?

I think at the time, it was a case of I was very happy doing what I was doing. The Under-21s were progressing well and we won the Toulon Tournament in the summer and we were very close to qualifying [for the Under-21 European Championships], so I wanted to finish that journey. When Roy left, I don't think there would have been a lot of support for an internal candidate at that moment. Whereas when Sam left, somebody had to step in and do the role immediately. There was no opportunity for me to think too much, it was a case that we needed leadership at that time and I felt that I was the best, most experienced person to do it. Then, once you have had a couple of games, people can see the way that you want to work and it gives you a chance to put some of your own ideas across. Then, I think there's a little bit more acceptance and support. Of course any manager needs internal support, but externally as well.

Since your appointment, you have encouragingly promoted youth and handed several players their senior international debuts. It seems you are planning for the future, as well as the present...?

It's natural for me to pick some of the younger players because I know them very well. I have worked with them and know what you're going to get from them. But equally, if people are playing well for their club and I think they fit into the style of play that we want to play, then I am not going to dismiss the opportunity for older players to play, like Jermain Defoe. There is a balance between getting results now and trying to build for the long-term.

What is the biggest influence you want to make on the senior England national team?

As a manager, I always want to allow the players to be as good as they might be. Try and tap into them expressing themselves. There's a lot that surrounds playing for England, it's not your day-to-day environment, so immediately it feels different for players. At club level, you can have 15 good games, then one not so good, but the supporters will remember the last 15. With England, you are judged on that one moment. People judge you immediately. It's a more pressured situation for players, but I have lived through that and I know what that needs, so the players don't need additional pressure or stress from me. My desire would be to create an environment where they feel more comfortable and relaxed and are able to play to their best.

What is your ultimate goal during your spell as Three Lions manager?

At the moment, we are ranked as number 13 in the world [June 2017] and our aim has got to become the best in the world. Everything we do in training, in preparation, what we eat and how we recover, we have got to ask ourselves, 'Is this going to make us a world-class team?' I think you have to focus on the bits you can control, so our preparation and the way the players prepare individually, but also how we prepare as a team. We have got to analyse what we can improve on from each performance and then results are a bi-product in the way we perform.

DID YOU KNOW?
Southgate captained Crystal Palace to the First Divison title [Championship] in 1994

Prior to your England roles, you also managed Middlesbrough between 2006 and 2009. Would you consider returning to club management in the future?

I'm not thinking of anything other than how I do this job as well as I possibly can. Club football, in terms of being a manager, was a huge learning experience for me. I had no coaching experience at all, but we did finish 12th and 13th in the Premier League. In the end, we were relegated. But, three years with no coaching experience was probably the biggest achievement of my life. In terms of life challenges, with such little experience, everything I was going into was new. In terms of career changes, that was the hardest by a million miles because everything else has been a gradual progression. The change from Under-21 to senior manager was no way near a bigger jump than going from playing to coaching. You have to focus on what is ahead of you and there is no reason for me to focus on anything else than England. It's a brilliant challenge and a great honour. I want to make sure, at whatever point it finishes, that I have dedicated absolutely everything that I have got to it.

What advice would you have for any young SHOOT readers who dream about playing for their country?

The fundamentals for me are work hard and continue to learn all the time. Always look to improve. Always work as hard and as smartly as you can. In any sport, the elite pathway comes with pressures and dynamic changes. But in the end, it's a game of football. Everybody starts because that's what they love doing. If you can enjoy it as much as you did when you first started playing and keep that sense of perspective, you're more likely to play well.

DID YOU KNOW?
Southgate remains Aston Villa's most capped England international player (42)

21 UNDER 21

YOURI TIELEMANS

Position: Midfielder
Date of Birth: May 7, 1997
National team: Belgium

AS Monaco's new signing had been lighting up the Belgian league with Anderlecht from the middle of the park for the past couple of years. Making a name for himself with some outstanding strikes from outside the box, the creative midfielder was handed the captain's armband at times last season at the age of just 19. The Belgians have produced some top players in recent years, however, Tielemans could well be the best yet.

FRANCK KESSIE

Position: Midfielder
Date of Birth: December 19, 1996
National team: Ivory Coast

Often compared to two-time Premier League champion Yaya Toure, fellow Ivory Coast international Kessie has been making quite the name for himself over the past year or so at Atalanta. Despite being deployed more often than not as a defensive midfielder, Kessie chipped in with an unusually high number of goals and assists for the Italian side last season, prompting Serie A giants AC Milan to sign him on a two-year loan deal.

CHRISTIAN PULISIC

Position: Midfielder
Date of Birth: September 18, 1998
National team: USA

The Borussia Dortmund playmaker moved from his home in Pennsylvania to join the German club's youth academy aged 15 and, after solving early work permit issues, quickly rose to be the most exciting prospect in American football for years. After just 15 appearances in the youth ranks, Pulisic made the step-up to the first-team and is now an established international and a key part of the first-team at Dortmund, with over 50 appearances to his name.

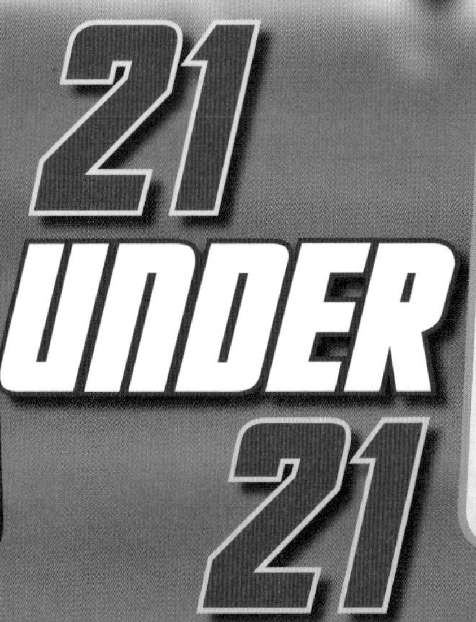

GIANLUIGI DONNARUMMA

Position: Goalkeeper
Date of Birth: February 25, 1999
National team: Italy

The Italian shot-stopper broke into the AC Milan team aged just 16, and has not looked back since. Astounding onlookers with saves well beyond his years, Donnarumma is being heralded as the natural success to Azzurri legend Gianluigi Buffon - quite the praise! With over 60 Serie A appearances under his belt, as well as senior international experience, the young goalkeeper is well on his way to becoming a European great.

ALEXANDER ISAK

Position: Striker
Date of Birth: September 21, 1999
National team: Sweden

A relative unknown this time last year, Swedish forward Isak is certainly one to watch out for over this season. Having had top clubs around Europe chasing his signature last year, the youngster opted to join Borussia Dortmund in January, and whilst he is yet to really get going in the first-team, his outstanding skill on the ball and finishing prowess will soon be lighting up the Bundesliga.

At *SHOOT*, we love nothing better than scouring Europe to find the top players to keep an eye out for. Whether they be starlets who are emerging here at home, or a talented youngster you're yet to notice making his mark on the continent, we've got it covered! With the 2018 FIFA World Cup just around the corner, some of Europe's brightest talents will be battling to get their name on their manager's 23-man list come the end of the season and have their very own breakthrough moment. Here are the 21 best players under-21 to keep an eye on this campaign.

KASPER DOLBERG

Position: Striker
Date of Birth: October 6, 1997
National team: Denmark

The Ajax striker well and truly exploded onto the scene during the 2016-17 season. The Denmark international made his competitive debut for the club in July 2016, marking the occasion with a goal against PAOK and followed suit in his full Eredivisie debut with a brace against Roda JC. Dolberg continued his fine form across the entire campaign, scoring 23 goals in 48 appearances in all competitions - not a bad way to introduce yourself!

TOM DAVIES

Position: Midfielder
Date of Birth: June 30, 1998
National team: England

Emerging from the Everton youth ranks under the guise of Dutch manager Ronald Koeman, Davies has come from nowhere to become one of the most exciting prospects in the Premier League. His deep Evertonian roots make him an instant hit with the fans at Goodison Park and this quick, creative play panders to the style that both manager and supporters wish for on Merseyside. Add into the mix the fact that his mum still drops him off at training, he has all the foundations to be a homegrown hero over the coming years.

BEN CHILWELL

Position: Defender
Date of Birth: December 21, 1996
National team: England

The Leicester City defender nearly joined Jurgen Klopp's Liverpool in the summer of 2016, but stayed put with the Premier League champions. Having battled injury in the early parts of the 2016-17 season, the England Under-21 international went on to impress in his cameo appearances, none more so than against La Liga giants Atletico Madrid in the UEFA Champions League quarter-final second leg.

RUBEN NEVES

Position: Midfielder
Date of Birth: March 13, 1997
National team: Portugal

Becoming the youngest ever captain in the UEFA Champions League aged just 18 for FC Porto, Neves has always been destined for big things. Whilst his role as a holding midfielder means the limelight will be shifted onto the more creative talents on this list, the Portuguese deserves just as much praise. Although tackles and interceptions are a key element of any defensive midfielder's game, Neves' ability to get things ticking from deep with his range of passing put him a cut above the rest.

OLIVER BURKE

Position: Midfielder
Date of Birth: April 7, 1997
National team: Scotland

Burke broke the mould as a British player in 2016 by making the move to Bundesliga side RB Leipzig, where he enjoyed a sensational debut season, finishing runners-up to champions Bayern Munich. The Scotland international is one for taking on his man out wide and is a dab hand when it comes to corners and free-kicks. Another campaign near the top of the German top-flight and we could well see one of Europe's big boys making a move.

BREEL EMBOLO

Position: Striker
Date of Birth: February 14, 1997
National team: Switzerland

The enigmatic FC Schalke forward missed most of his first season with the German side through injury, but showed enough in his early games and his time with FC Basel that he has more than enough to become one of Europe's greats. The Switzerland international, who possesses strength beyond his years as well as blistering pace, is a versatile attacker who can operate anywhere along the midfield or frontline.

KYLIAN MBAPPE

Position: Striker
Date of Birth: December 20, 1998
National team: France

No player epitomised the rise of last season's Ligue 1 champions, AS Monaco, more than young forward Mbappe. Scoring one goal in his first campaign with the senior squad in 2015-16, it was fair to say no one expected the Frenchman to explode as he did under Leonardo Jardim over the last twelve months, scoring 26 goals and playing a key role in getting to the semi-finals of the UEFA Champions League.

RENATO SANCHES

Position: Midfielder
Date of Birth: August 18, 1997
National team: Portugal

The explosive Portuguese midfielder really made a name for himself at Euro 2016, making six appearances, including the final, on his way to lifting the trophy alongside captain Cristiano Ronaldo. A technically masterful player, Sanches loves to take on his opponents and more often than not is clear of them with a flick or a sly drop of the shoulder. Despite not enjoying the best of seasons after a big-money move to Bayern Munich, the youngster has all the tools to develop into one of the top midfielders in world football.

OUSMANE DEMBELE

Position: Midfielder
Date of Birth: May 15, 1997
National team: France

The pacey forward more than made his mark in the Bundesliga with Borussia Dortmund last season as a key part of a pack of exciting young players. The Frenchman, who also has a knack when it comes to set pieces, can be relied upon to create chances aplenty for those ahead of him, having ranked amongst the top assist providers in Germany last term.

GABRIEL JESUS

Position: Striker
Date of Birth: April 3, 1997
National team: Brazil

Winning Olympic gold at Rio 2016, Jesus attracted the attention of the newly appointed Manchester City boss Pep Guardiola as he looked to build a strike force for the future. The 20-year-old had to wait until the New Year to make his Citizens debut, but he arrived in scintillating style, even ousting Sergio Aguero from the teamsheet, after scoring seven goals in just 11 outings. His pace, quick feet and eye for goal will serve City well for years to come.

EMRE MOR

Position: Midfielder
Date of Birth: July 24, 1997
National team: Turkey

Turkish international Mor became another youth hopeful at Borussia Dortmund when he joined the German side from Danish club FC Nordsjaelland in 2016 and, although he had to endure an injury hit debut term, he has all the qualities to go straight to the top. The young playmaker, who is never afraid to take on his marker with a little bit of skill, has an eye for a clever pass or key ball and could well be a player the Bundesliga outfit look to build their team around in years to come.

RIECHEDLY BAZOER

Position: Midfielder
Date of Birth: October 12, 1996
National team: Netherlands

The solid Netherlands midfielder moved from his home country to join Wolfsburg in the Bundesliga earlier this year, and hasn't looked back, firmly establishing himself in the side under manager Andries Jonker. Whilst keeping things tight in the middle, the Dutch international can still turn things around and have a strong influence on things going forward, often retrieving the ball and starting attacks from deep – certainly one for the future!

GONCALO GUEDES

Position: Midfielder
Date of Birth: November 29, 1996
National team: Portugal

The Portuguese playmaker left his hometown club Benfica in January 2017 after impressing scouts at Paris Saint-Germain, and is very much working his way into the side in the French capital. A nightmare to get the ball from for any defender, the youngster can create the perfect chance in the blink of an eye when sitting in his favoured No.10 position, and will undoubtedly emerge as one of the top talents at PSG over the next few years.

KELECHI IHEANACHO

Position: Striker
Date of Birth: October 3, 1996
National team: Nigeria

Another top striker from the Manchester City ranks, Iheanacho has an eye for goal unlike many others his age. In the shadow of Sergio Aguero, and now Gabriel Jesus, during his rise at The Etihad Stadium, the Nigerian has still managed to dazzle and impress when called upon. Whether he needs to take on his man in the box or make a clever run to latch onto a cross, you can more than trust Iheanacho to get the job done.

ANTE CORIC

Position: Midfielder
Date of Birth: April 14, 1997
National team: Croatia

The Croatian midfielder has been tearing it up in his home country for quite some time now, having already notched up well over 100 first-team appearances for Dinamo Zagreb, including some significant outings in the UEFA Champions League. A tricky man to keep track of if you're lining up against him, Coric has often been compared to Real Madrid star and compatriot, Luka Modric. Again, no pressure there then!

MARCUS RASHFORD

Position: Striker
Date of Birth: October 31, 1997
National team: England

There is little left to say about Rashford. The debut specialist has taken on the mantle of Manchester United wonderkid in fine style and is arguably the player on which fans at Old Trafford have pinned the future of the club on – no pressure! The England international took the burden on replacing Zlatan Ibrahimovic at the end of last season in his stride and has a habit of making his mark on only the biggest of games.

10 THINGS YOU DIDN'T KNOW ABOUT...

Antoine

Behind Lionel Messi and Cristiano Ronaldo, many view France superstar Antoine Griezmann as the best player in Europe. The forward has been one of the most prolific forwards in the continent following his move to Atletico Madrid in 2014, where he scored 26 goals in 53 appearances for the La Liga outfit in 2016-17. The striker also showcased his stunning goalscoring form with six goals at Euro 2016, taking home the Golden Boot. The 26-year-old has performed at the top level for several years now, for both club and country, but how well do you really know Griezmann? Here are 10 things you probably didn't know about the France forward...

PROFILE

HEIGHT: 1.75m
DATE OF BIRTH: March 21,1991
PLACE OF BIRTH: Macon, France
NATIONAL TEAM: France

Griezmann

1. He wears Spongebob Squarepants underwear on matchdays, which he deems are a 'lucky charm'.

2. Griezmann is a huge fan of the South American drink 'maté' – a caffeine-rich beverage which he has every morning to get his day going.

3. When he was 11-years-old, Griezmann would train every Wednesday at French side Lyon. But the club never chose to sign him because of his size.

4. Ironically, Griezmann scored a remarkable overhead kick to help Real Sociedad knock Lyon out of the UEFA Champions League play-off round in 2013.

5. Griezmann admits he models his game on Spain and Manchester City star David Silva.

6. Former England captain David Beckham is Griezmann's idol and the reason behind his preferred No.7 shirt.

7. When Griezmann made his senior debut for France back in 2014, he sang his initiation song in Spanish, having played for Real Sociedad since the age of 14.

8. Griezmann was banned for over a year from representing France at any international level back in 2012 after he and several Under-21 team-mates went out partying instead of reporting for training!

of

9. He once played with Arsenal on Football Manager and went onto win the Premier League title and Champions League. Watch out Arsene Wenger!

10. Griezmann has won more La Liga Player of the Month Awards (four) than both Cristiano Ronaldo and Lionel Messi (both two) since its introduction in 2013.

STADIUM QUIZ

1

Ground:
Team:
Capacity:

2

Ground:
Team:
Capacity:

3

Ground:
Team:
Capacity:

4

Ground:
Team:
Capacity:

Anfield – Liverpool – 54,074
Celtic Park – Celtic – 60,411
Emirates Stadium – Arsenal – 60,432
Etihad Stadium – Manchester City – 55,097

'THE BEAUTIFUL GAME' IS PLAYED INSIDE SOME OF THE MOST SPECTACULAR STADIUMS IN WORLD FOOTBALL. BUT, HOW MUCH DO YOU KNOW ABOUT THE UNITED KINGDOM'S GREATEST GROUNDS? *SHOOT* VISITED EIGHT OF THE BEST VENUES, ALL YOU HAVE TO DO IS NAME THE STADIUM, WRITE DOWN WHICH CLUB PLAYS THERE AND CORRECTLY GUESS ITS CAPACITY. GOOD LUCK!

5

Ground:

Team:

Capacity:

6

Ground:

Team:

Capacity:

7

Ground:

Team:

Capacity:

8

Ground:

Team:

Capacity:

London Stadium – West Ham United – 66,000
Old Trafford – Manchester United – 75,643
St James' Park – Newcastle United – 52,405
Wembley Stadium – Tottenham Hotspur – 90,000

CHECK YOUR ANSWERS ON PAGE 77!

Retro Replay: MICHAEL OWEN

We have rolled back the years to recreate an interview with former Liverpool, Real Madrid, Newcastle United and Manchester United striker Michael Owen.

The 37-year-old, who sits eighth in the all-time Premier League goalscoring charts with 150 strikes, spoke exclusively to *SHOOT* nearly 20 years on from his January 1998 interview to answer those all important questions again and reminisce about his career's greatest moments.

In 1997, you were voted *SHOOT's* Young Player of the Year. What was the best honour you ever won?

The 2001 FA Cup. That day, we were losing 1-0 to Arsenal and then I scored two in the last few minutes. That's just what I did for ten years as a kid in the back garden, commentating to myself, Owen scoring the winning goal in the FA Cup final and running around the garden. That's just what dreams were made of. If I could live one day again in my career, I think that FA Cup final was a magical day. But from a personal point of view, winning the Ballon d'Or. Even my kids think their dad is quite cool when you look at the greats that have won it.

Glenn Hoddle handed you your England debut against Chile in February 1998, aged 18. What can you remember from that day?

It was amazing. To be told you were going to play for your country, it was all such a whirlwind at the time. Chile won 2-0, but I didn't feel really disappointed, I was just so proud of playing for my country. I think I got Man of the Match as well!

What was your favourite moment playing for The Three Lions?

I think scoring that goal against Argentina (1998 FIFA World Cup) turned me from sort of a domestic name into a worldwide name. That changed my life in many ways. So to score that goal, on the biggest stage against a huge team, was probably the highlight.

DID YOU KNOW?

Owen is the youngest player to reach 100 goa in the Premier League

MY ENGLAND

He's only 18, but Michael C storm this season, upstag Anfield scoring stakes and the England squad. SHOO

When SHOOT met up with Michael Owen last September, he told us his ambition for the coming season was to play in as many first-team games as possible.

It speaks volumes for the youngster's amazing footie ability that now, four months later, he's talking about the possibility of a call-up to the full England side, having already played for the Under-21s as a 17-year-old! And even though England boss Glenn Hoddle is keen to play down talk of Mikey going to France '98, no-one will be surprised if he pips the likes of Ian Wright and Robbie Fowler into the final 22 man squad.

To round off a great year for Michael, SHOOT readers voted him their Young Player Of The Year for 1997. In the poll Mikey finished miles ahead of Beckham and Scholes, who had both won the Prem with Man United and were regulars in the England side, suggesting that a new footie superstar was about to be born!

So SHOOT met up with Michael to discuss his first major award, the punishment he takes off defenders, being in the spotlight at such a young age and getting sent-off playing for England.

OWEN SPECIAL

CUP DREAM

I hopefully make that step up to the full squad.

WERE YOU OVERAWED TRAINING WITH THE FULL SQUAD?

Not really. I train with a lot of those players every day at club level and I didn't feel out of my depth at all. It's a great experience for a young lad like me to go and train with the full-squad and every one of the England lads has been very

DID YOU KNOW?

Owen never scored against Liverpool during his career, despite facing the reds five times. However, he netted 13 times against fellow former club Newcastle United, which is more goals than he managed against any other club

After reaching the semi-finals of Euro 1996, should England have performed better at major tournaments during your international career?

Yeah I think so, certainly with those 1998 and 2000 teams. But I was lucky to play in two of the best England teams that we had for a long, long time. Then the new generation of promise, the likes of [Rio] Ferdinand, [Steven] Gerrard, [David] Beckham, [Paul] Scholes, [Ashley] Cole, [John] Terry and [Wayne] Rooney, it was top quality. It was a crying shame that we never won anything with any of those.

You went onto score 158 goals in 297 appearances for Liverpool overall. Did you ever see yourself becoming a Reds legend?

When you start playing, you don't ever think about what is going to happen at the end. But I was always top of my class, I was probably the best player in the country from 12-years-old, all the way through, so I was always at the top of my game. I definitely expected to be a top class football player. I would be lying otherwise if I said I didn't.

Do you regret leaving Liverpool for Real Madrid back in 2004?

If I said no to Real Madrid, I would have always wondered what it would have been like to play in that kit, the stadium, a different league, with [Zinedine] Zidane, [Luis] Figo, Ronaldo and Beckham. I would have always been thinking, 'I had the opportunity, but I said no'. The plan was to always come back. I regret not playing for Liverpool again.

***SHOOT* picked up upon you being sent off for the first time in your career after headbutting Yugoslavia Under-18 defender Sead Muratovic in 1997. Do you remember what happened?**

I was getting man marked and he kept fouling me. I was on the floor and he stood over me as if to have a go at me. So I just jumped up, and my head thrashed up into his chest. I got sent off for it unfortunately. That was a big learning curve for me!

What advice would you have for any *SHOOT* readers who want to become the next Michael Owen?

The bottom line is that you have got to have a lot of ability to start off with.. Once you have got that ability, then you can start talking about mental strength and belief, the different things you have got to do to improve your game. I'm not one for thinking that everybody has got to improve on weaknesses. I think if you have got one or two strengths, then it's great being the best at two things. You have got to set yourself apart from everybody else, whatever your attribute is.

You haven't headbutted anyone since, right...?

[Laughs] I wouldn't class it as a headbutt. But yeah, it's the first and last time!

MIDFIELDER
DID YOU KNOW?
Pogba became the first Premier League star to get an official Twitter hashtag emoji in January 2017.
PAUL POGBA
CLUB:
MANCHESTER UNITED
HEIGHT: 1.91M
DATE OF BIRTH:
March 15, 1993
PLACE OF BIRTH:
LAGNY-SUR-MARNE, FRANCE
NATIONAL TEAM:
FRANCE
adidas
CHEVROLET

PEDRO

CLUB: CHELSEA
HEIGHT: 1.67M
DATE OF BIRTH:
July 28, 1987
PLACE OF BIRTH:
SANTA CRUZ DE TENERIFE, SPAIN
NATIONAL TEAM:
SPAIN

DID YOU KNOW?

Pedro didn't begin his professional career until he was 17 after impressing Barcelona scouts whilst playing for local club CD San Isidro.

LEAGUE OF LEGENDS

SHOOT takes a look at each Premier League club's all-time hero...

Credit: AFC Bournemouth

Steve Fletcher

The Cherries hero scored 121 goals in 728 games over two spells with the club spanning 18 years. However, his most memorable moment in a AFC Bournemouth shirt came against Grimsby Town in 2009, completing the club's Great Escape from relegation of the Football League.

Thierry Henry

The French sensation is known for bagging outstanding goals across Europe, nowhere more so, however, than at Arsenal. Over two spells with the club, firstly from 1999-2007 before returning on loan in 2012, the bewildering striker scored a club record 228 goals in 377 games for The Gunners.

Jimmy McIlroy MBE

A footballing hall of famer, Jimmy McIlroy scored 131 goals in 497 appearances for Burnley between 1950 and 1963. The former Clarets forward, who has a stand at Turf Moor named after him, was an integral part of the 1959-60 side which won the First Division.

Gary Stevens

The defender, or Grease as he is known by fans, made his debut aged 17 and was an instant hit, making 26 appearances in his first season. Stevens made over 130 appearances for Brighton, including in the club's first appearance in an FA Cup final, in which the defender scored their only goal.

Credit: Burnley FC

Frank Lampard

'Super Frank', as he is fondly known in West London is arguably the best midfielder to have graced the Premier League. The UEFA Champions League winner scored an astonishing 211 goals in 649 appearances for The Blues between 2001-2014.

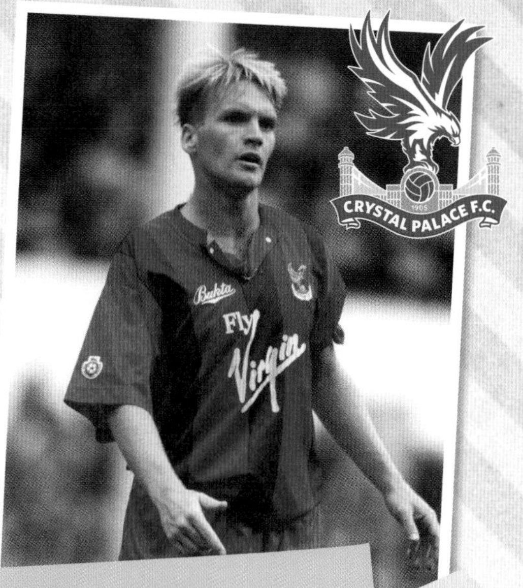

Geoff Thomas

Thomas scored 35 goals in 249 appearances for The Eagles between 1987 and 1993. The midfielder captained the side in both the 1990 FA Cup final defeat to Manchester United, as well as the Zenith Data Systems Cup triumph against Everton the year after.

Dixie Dean

Dean is a true Everton legend. In his 12 years at the club from 1925-1937, he scored 383 goals, more than any single player has ever scored for one club in English football. The striker also holds the record for most goals in one English top-flight season, with 60 strikes in 1927-28.

Andy Booth

Across two spells between 1992–1996 and 2001–2009, the homegrown striker fans call 'The Legend' scored 150 goals in 457 appearances for The Terriers. In his first spell with the club, Booth scored in both the play-off semi-finals and final to earn promotion to Division One in 1995.

Steve Walsh

Once voted Leicester City's all-time 'hard man', Walsh made 450 appearances for The Foxes from 1986–2000. He was named Man of the Match in the 1997 League Cup final draw with Middlesbrough and in the replay win ten days later.

Kenny Dalglish

'King Kenny' as he is known at Anfield scored 172 goals in 515 appearances before taking the helm as manager on two occasions. Overall the Scotsman won nine league titles, three European Cups, three FA Cups, five League Cups and one UEFA Super Cup.

Colin Bell

Adored by fans in the blue half of Manchester, 'the King' made 498 appearances for City from 1966–1979. During his time with The Citizens, Bell won the First Division, Second Division, the FA Cup, the League Cup and the European Cup Winners' Cup.

Sir Bobby Charlton

One of just nine players to survive the 1958 Munich air disaster, Charlton embodies everything Manchester United stands for as a club. The 1966 FIFA World Cup winner made 758 appearances for The Red Devils from 1956-1973, scoring 249 goals, a record which was only broken last season by Wayne Rooney.

Alan Shearer

The Premier League's all-time top goalscorer with 260 goals, 148 of which came at Newcastle United, Shearer is a true Geordie legend. With 206 goals in all competitions for The Magpies across ten years with the club, his brief managerial spell at the club will never be held against him at St James' Park.

Matt Le Tissier

This one-club man donned the famous No.7 shirt for The Saints and had more than a few teams built around him. 'Le God,' as he is known to those down south, scored 209 goals in the red and white stripes of Southampton - 47 of which were penalties, missing just one!

Sir Stanley Matthews

Across two spells with the club between 1932–1947 and 1961–1965, he scored 62 goals in 355 appearances. Matthews is remembered most fondly for the longevity of his career, most shown with his two honours at Stoke, winning the Second Division twice, with 30 years in between.

Ivor Allchurch

The 'Golden Boy' of Welsh football is Swansea City's all-time top goalscorer with 166 goals for 445 appearances. The forward, who represented Wales at the 1958 World Cup, left The Swans in 1958, before returning for a second spell in 1965.

Danny Blanchflower

Tottenham's 1961 League and Cup double winning captain scored 21 goals in 382 appearances for the North London club over a 10-year spell. As well as the double triumph, the midfielder lifted a second FA Cup a year later and the European Cup Winners' Cup the following season.

Luther Blissett

The Jamaica-born striker racked up 503 appearances for Watford, more than any other player, across three spells with the club between 1975–1983, 1984–1988 and 1991–1993. As well as topping the appearance charts for The Hornets, Blissett also holds the record for most goals scored, after netting 186 in all competitions.

Ronnie Allen

A winger turned striker, Allen spent 11 years with The Baggies from 1950-1961, winning the FA Cup in 1954 and finished second in the First Division the same season. The England international scored 234 goals in 458 appearances for West Brom, before twice going on to lead the club as manager.

Bobby Moore

The 1966 FIFA World Cup winning England captain made an astonishing 646 appearances for The Irons between 1958-1974. The defender also captained West Ham for over a decade and, 15 years after his death, retired his famous No.6 shirt in 2008.

GUARDIOLA'S S

Barcelona have MSN [Lionel Messi, Luis Suarez and Neymar], Manchester United have their United Trinity of George Best, Denis Law and Sir Bobby Charlton, the Father, the Son and the Holy Spirit combine to make the Holy Trininty and in the blue half of Manchester, Pep Guardiola has begun work on a trinity of his own.

The arrival of Gabriel Jesus at The Etihad Stadium in January marked the dawn of a new era for The Citizens.

The Spanish manager had spent the first-half of the season bringing the best out of Raheem Sterling, whilst also getting summer signing Leroy Sane settled in the Premier League. Add Jesus to the mix, and we were all about to witness something special.

"The dawn of a new era for The Citizens"

Ever since Guardiola arrived in the English game, there has been a sense that he is clearing out at The Etihad. The arrival of John Stones, as well as Sane and Jesus in his first summer, showed that the former Barcelona boss was looking to youth to take his side forward, and the same can be said of his second summer of business in England.

The realisation of just how good these three young forwards, who combine with an average age of 21, are when playing together came when Jesus made his first league start in a City shirt.

Lining up against West Ham United at the London Stadium, where the Mancunians had won 5-0 just weeks before, the three combined devastatingly during their 4-0 mauling of The Hammers, with Jesus netting his first Premier League goal inside his first full half of action, with all three involved in the build-up.

With the experience and tact of David Silva and Kevin De Bruyne behind them, the trio can cause untold havoc against opposition defences with each of the stars bringing their own attributes which dovetail perfectly.

PER STRIKEFORCE

Out on the right, Sterling has flourished under the guise of Guardiola and enjoyed arguably his best season in the Premier League in 2016-17. The City manager has added a new level of understanding and vision to the pace and skill which underpins Sterling's game, making the England international ever more dangerous to face as an opposing defender.

On the opposite flank, having arrived from Germany last summer and been slowly nurtured into a starter over the first-half of the campaign, Sane took the Premier League by storm in 2017. The blistering pace of the No.19 has made a mockery of full-backs up and down the country.

The former Schalke man is alarmingly intelligent for a player of his age and has shown as much with his split second decision-making in and around the penalty area, more than happy to set-up a team-mate, as he is to go for goal himself.

That, then, leaves the final prong in this destructive, enigmatic, young trinity - Jesus. Having had to wait until January to play, after finalising his move to England from Palmeiras, many would have forgiven the youngster if he had taken a while to get going. However, the Brazilian, who won Olympic Gold at Rio 2016, alongside Neymar, hit the ground running and even managed to unseat one of the finest goalscorers in Premier League history, Sergio Aguero, in doing so.

Having seen just a glimpse of the damage these three can do when they line up alongside one another, it's clear that Pep has a plan to take the three pronged attack which served him so well on the continent to a new level in the Premier League with this newborn trinity. There is plenty more to come!

MEGA QUIZ

1.

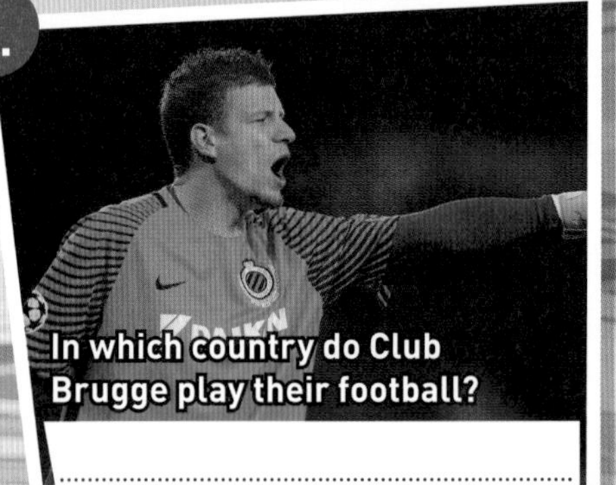

In which country do Club Brugge play their football?

2.

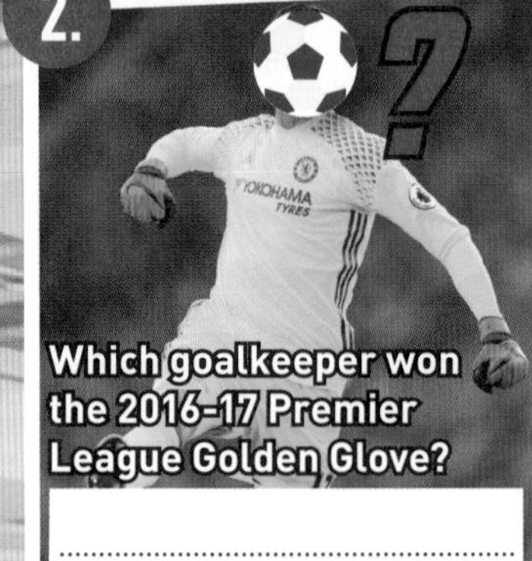

Which goalkeeper won the 2016-17 Premier League Golden Glove?

3.

What year did England win the FIFA World Cup?

4.

Who did England defeat in the 2015 FIFA Women's World Cup third place play-off?

5.

From which club did Manchester City sign Bernardo Silva?

6.

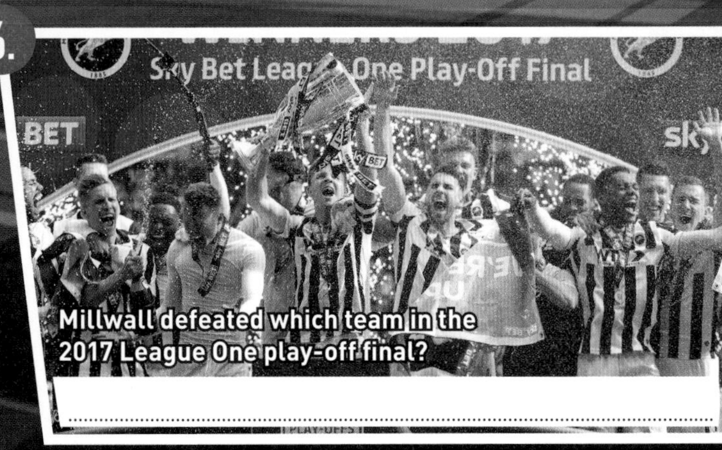

Millwall defeated which team in the 2017 League One play-off final?

7.

Arsenal, Chelsea, Manchester City and which other club has won the Women's Super League 1 title?

8.

At which club did Theo Walcott begin his senior career?

9.

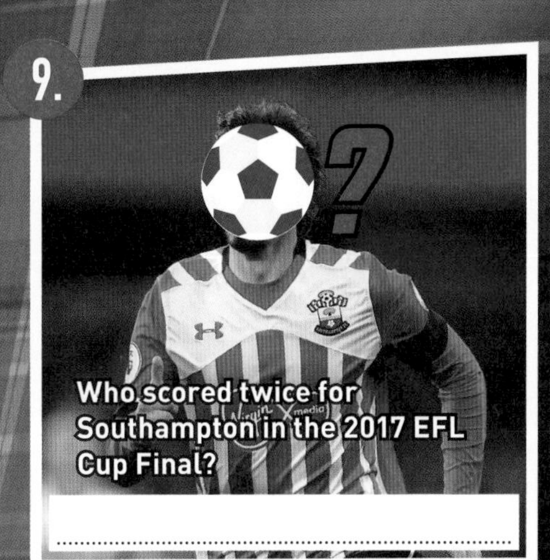

Who scored twice for Southampton in the 2017 EFL Cup Final?

10.

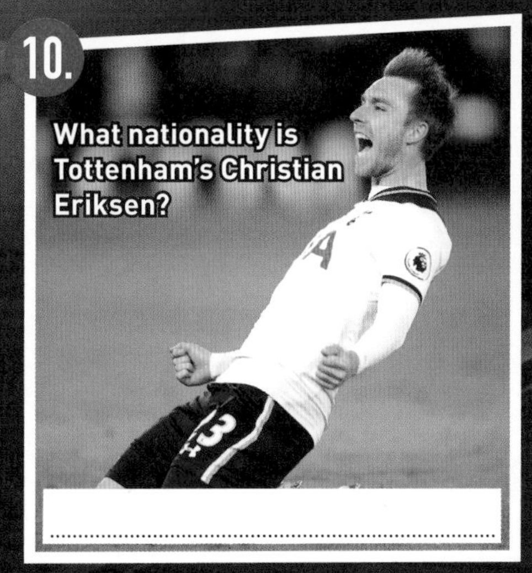

What nationality is Tottenham's Christian Eriksen?

11.

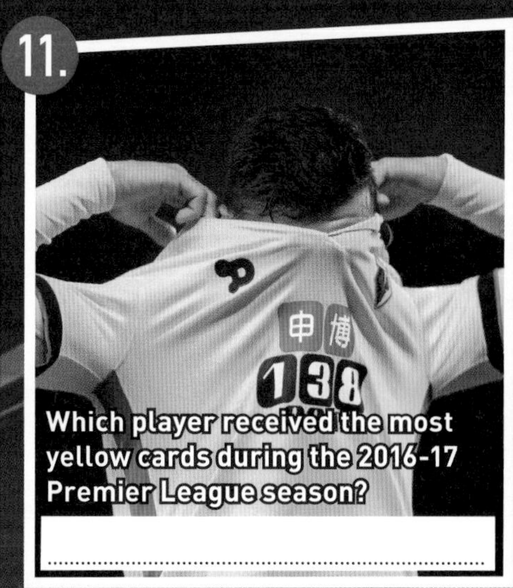

Which player received the most yellow cards during the 2016-17 Premier League season?

12.

Celtic boss Brendan Rodgers used to manage Liverpool, Swansea City and which other Premier League club?

13.

Whose club badge is this?

14.

What is Sunderland's nickname?

15.

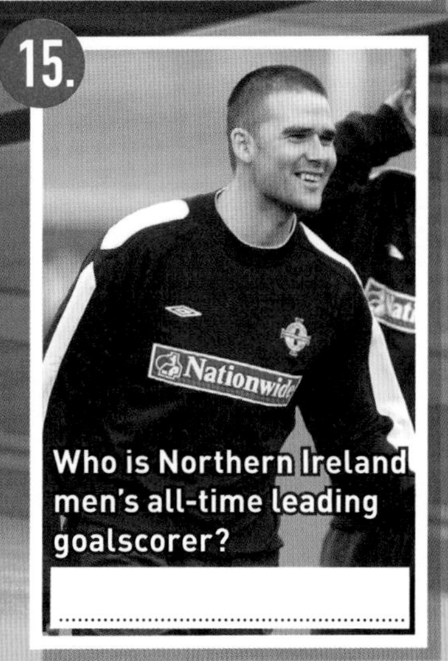

Who is Northern Ireland men's all-time leading goalscorer?

16.

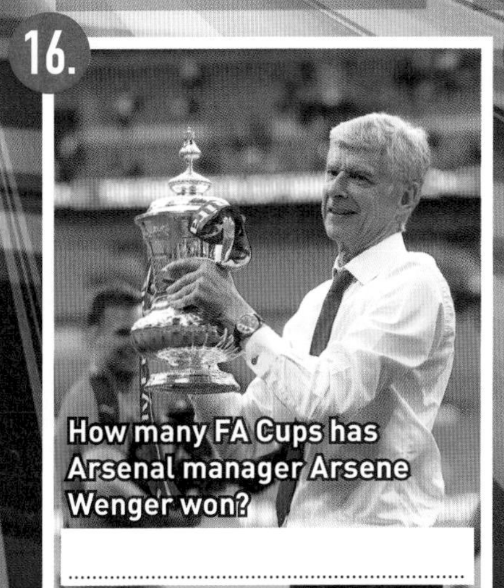

How many FA Cups has Arsenal manager Arsene Wenger won?

17.

England boss Gareth Southgate used to manage which former Premier League club?

18.

Which non-league club reached the quarter-finals of the FA Cup in 2017?

19.

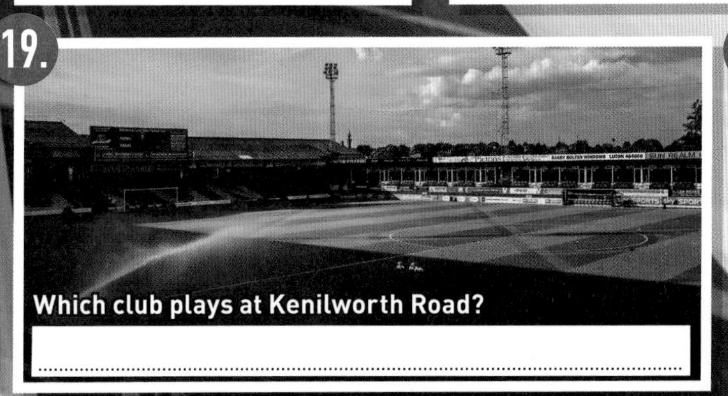

Which club plays at Kenilworth Road?

20.

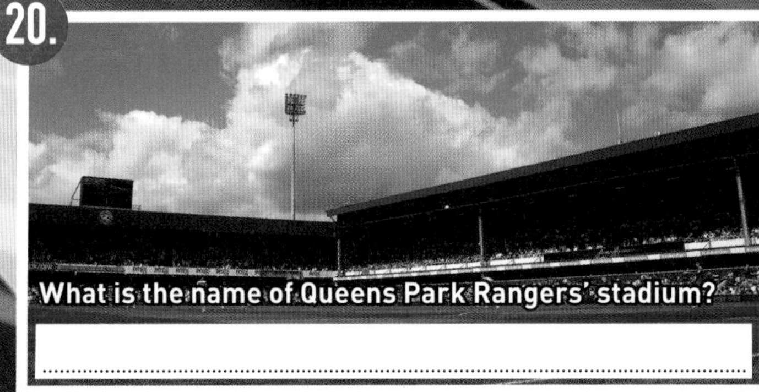

What is the name of Queens Park Rangers' stadium?

CHECK ALL OF YOUR ANSWERS ON PAGE 77!

FACT FILE

NAME: Eniola Aluko
POSITION: Striker
HEIGHT: 1.59m
DATE OF BIRTH:
February 21, 1987
PLACE OF BIRTH:
Lagos, Nigeria
CLUBS: Birmingham City Ladies, Charlton Athletic Ladies, Saint Louis Athletica, Atlanta Beat, Sky Blue FC, Chelsea Ladies

Aluko supported Manchester United during her childhood and was a huge fan of Eric Cantona – even popping her collar like the Frenchman!

ENIOLA ALUKO

From being the only girl playing in a boys' team, to not being selected for UEFA Euro 2017, Eniola Aluko is no stranger to harsh treatment, but she has overcome every obstacle thrown at her to become one of England's greatest ever strikers.
Despite winning the FA Women's Super League 1 Golden Boot last season, scoring nine goals from just 13 starts, the Chelsea striker was overlooked for The Lionesses' squad in the Netherlands this summer - the first time in 12 years Aluko was not selected for her country at a major tournament.

SHOOT spoke exclusively to the 30-year-old forward about her career challenges, greatest games, her England exile and life after football.

HOW DID YOUR JOURNEY IN FOOTBALL BEGIN?

I grew up in Birmingham and I was the only girl in the local area that played. Football was my way of being accepted, because I was the odd one out as the only girl. Then I actually realised I was really good at it, probably better than some of the boys. I was the only girl in my boys' team. Parents would actually say it was against the rules for me to play. That was hard for me. I felt like being a girl footballer was wrong and not accepted. Luckily when I was 12, I told my mum I wanted to play for a girls' team, so I didn't feel left out, and I realised that there were actually loads of girls just like me.

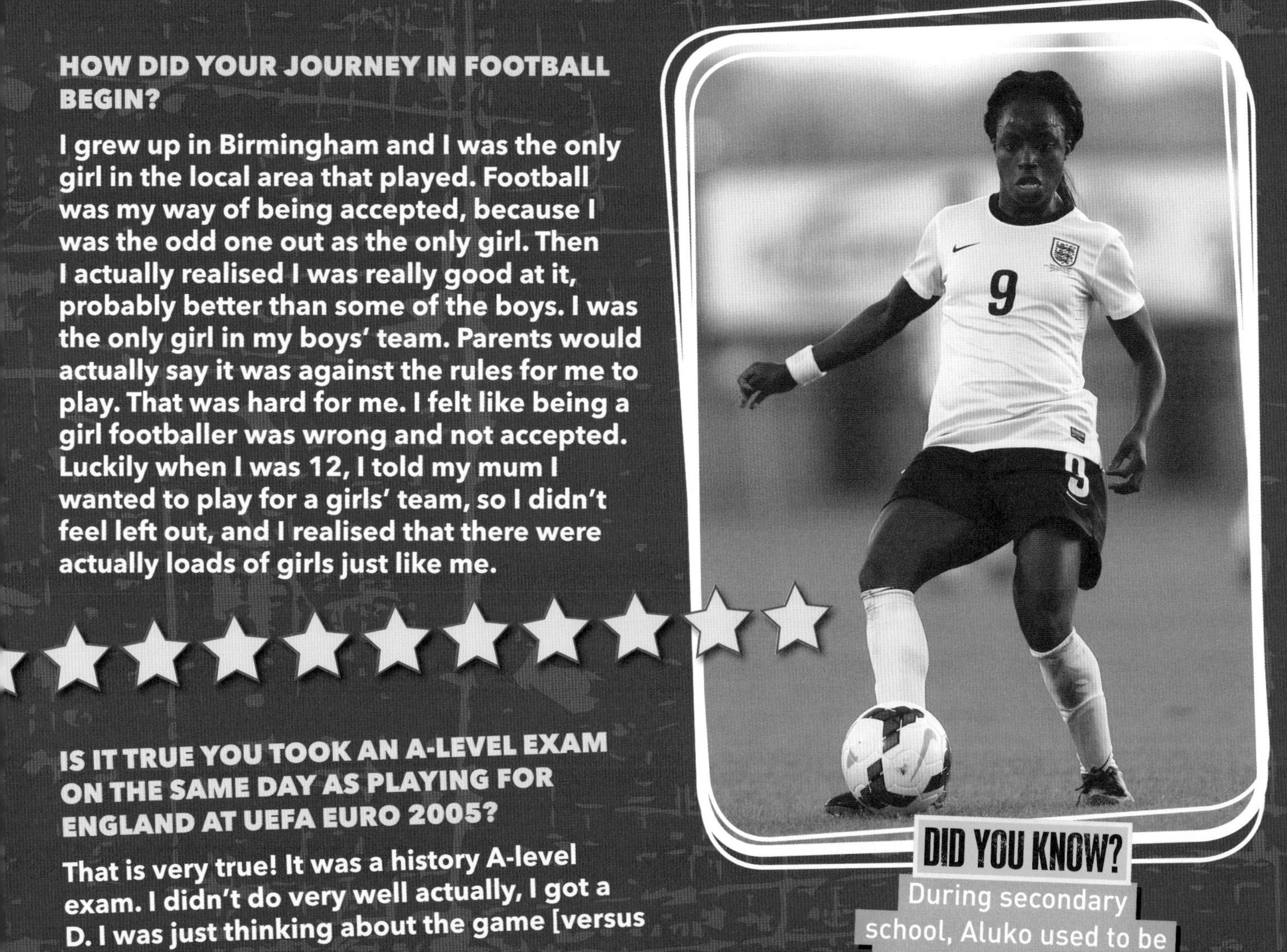

IS IT TRUE YOU TOOK AN A-LEVEL EXAM ON THE SAME DAY AS PLAYING FOR ENGLAND AT UEFA EURO 2005?

That is very true! It was a history A-level exam. I didn't do very well actually, I got a D. I was just thinking about the game [versus Finland]!

DID YOU KNOW?

During secondary school, Aluko used to be the lead singer in her local church choir

DIDN'T YOU JUGGLE YOUR FOOTBALL CAREER WITH UNIVERSITY, BEFORE MAKING IT PROFESSIONALLY?

Yes, I went to Brunel University London and studied law. There wasn't a clear pathway as a professional footballer, at that time. There was no such thing as a professional team, apart from Fulham Ladies, but I didn't feel I was going to get into that team. I'm really interested in the business side of running a football club. Because of my legal background, I understand the contracts, sports governance, the club's perspective and also the player's view. Naturally, if I were to go into a club director role, there would be very similar legal requirements that I would understand. I look back now and I'm really grateful that I did go to university.

YOU WERE THE FIRST-EVER FEMALE PUNDIT ON MATCH OF THE DAY. HAVE YOU GOT AN EYE ON MORE MEDIA WORK IN THE NEAR FUTURE?

It's something I would like to do when I stop playing too. It was amazing. I was really nervous because no women had done it before and I just wanted to come across as a good pundit, not a good female pundit. I wanted to come across as if I knew what I was talking about, so people could go, 'Oh, well she knows what she is talking about!' Why shouldn't we be on the show? I really enjoyed it and thankfully other people enjoyed it as well. I did the men's Euros [2016] and women's Euros [2017], so hopefully in the future I can do a men's World Cup and the Olympics.

YOU WERE PART OF THE FIRST TEAM GB WOMEN'S FOOTBALL SQUAD. WHAT ARE YOUR MEMORIES FROM THE LONDON 2012 OLYMPIC GAMES?

That was an amazing experience, and one that's unique, because I don't know whether we will ever play in an Olympics again. Doing it at a home Olympics was life changing. I remember going to the Olympic Village and getting in a lift with Mo Farah. I was like, "Oh my God, it is Mo Farah!" I think it was a watershed moment for women's football in this country. It made people really sit up and think, 'Actually this is a great product on the pitch'.

ENGLAND RECORDED THEIR BEST-EVER WOMEN'S WORLD CUP FINISH WITH A BRONZE MEDAL BACK IN 2015. WHAT WAS IT LIKE BEING PART OF THAT SQUAD?

We were actually cocooned away from all of the noise when we were actually out there. But when we came back, it was absolutely massive. We didn't realise how much people really got behind it and I think the viewing figures were comparable to the men's viewing figures. I think a lot of young girls were inspired by the women's team and I think the attendances were doubled as a result directly after.

DID YOU KNOW?

Aluko is fifth in the all-time leading goalscoring charts for England Women with 33 strikes

DID YOU KNOW?

Aluko was the first female pundit to appear on Match of the Day

BEATING GERMANY IN THE PLAY-OFF AND FINISHING THIRD IN THE WORLD CUP. IS THAT THE PROUDEST MOMENT OF YOUR CAREER?

No, I wouldn't say it's the proudest moment. I like to win! But beating Germany was amazing. My proudest moment is winning the FA Cup for Chelsea. That was the first women's FA Cup final at Wembley. Then a few months later, we won the league, that was my first league title in my career.

YOU'VE BEEN CRITICAL OF ENGLAND MANAGER MARK SAMPSON'S SELECTION POLICY AND MISSED OUT ON THE LIONESSES' EURO 2017 SQUAD. HOW DID YOU TAKE THE OMISSION?

I wasn't expecting to get picked because I hadn't been picked for over a year, despite scoring a lot of goals for club and country. Plus, I hadn't spoken to the manager for over 12 months. I was only disappointed because I think every player wants to feel like your performances mean something. I think it raised questions for many people, whether the squad was picked on merit before a ball had even been kicked in the Spring Series. For my nine-year-old little brother asking me why I wasn't picked, even though I scored loads of goals, that's a very difficult conversation. He wants to be going out playing for his local team and think, 'If I play well, I'll get picked' because that's what my sister did. I think it was important for me to actually say what many were thinking and reiterate to people, especially young people, that hard work and performance should matter above anything else.

ARE YOU STILL HOPEFUL OF RETURNING TO THE ENGLAND SET-UP ONE DAY?

I have moved on. I have alluded to it. It's not about looking back and feeling bitter about anything. I have got over 100 caps, so I can't really complain. I have had 11 years of playing for my national team and hopefully everytime I put that shirt on, I made people proud. If this is the end, it's the end. If it's not, I think under another manager, potentially we'll wait and see.

HAVE YOU THOUGHT ABOUT RETIRING FROM INTERNATIONAL DUTY?

I have, but I don't think now is the right time. As much as I think the door is shut, I would like to leave it a little bit open. So we'll see.

YOU WON THE WOMEN'S SUPER LEAGUE 1 GOLDEN BOOT LAST YEAR. WOULD YOU SAY YOU'RE CURRENTLY IN THE BEST FORM OF YOUR CAREER?

I think I am! I'm mentally strong as I have ever been and physically I'm always getting better too. It's very difficult to get into a rhythm at Chelsea, because there's a lot of competition, so I can only be as good as I'm allowed to be. I can't score goals from the bench! But I will train and work hard to keep getting better so I can perform for my team.

HAVING WON NUMEROUS HONOURS FOR CLUB AND COUNTRY, WHAT IS YOUR NEXT ULTIMATE AIM?

The UEFA Champions League. I think if I were to win that, I'll probably retire the next day! I want to win the league again. I want to win the FA Cup again. If I can do all of that by the time I have packed it all in, then I'll be very happy.

WHAT THREE TIPS DO YOU HAVE FOR ANY *SHOOT* READERS WANTING TO BECOME THE NEXT ENIOLA ALUKO?

1. Always look to perform. Every opportunity you are given to train or play well, make sure your main focus is how you perform. If you are given a role or responsibility, try to do it to the best of your ability.
2. Understand that failure is a huge part of success. It can be a great platform to succeed, but a lot of people really let it get to them. It's about using that failure, getting back up and making sure you come back stronger.
3. The other thing is sacrifice. Young people can get very distracted. Football can be lonely sometimes. You have to eat well, can't drink and can't go out partying. If you really want to achieve in football, you have to put all of that aside.

JAMIE VARDY

CLUB:
LEICESTER CITY
HEIGHT: 1.78M
DATE OF BIRTH:
January 11, 1987
PLACE OF BIRTH:
SHEFFIELD, ENGLAND
NATIONAL TEAM:
ENGLAND

DID YOU KNOW?

Vardy holds the record for scoring in the most consecutive Premier League matches – netting 13 goals in 11 games.

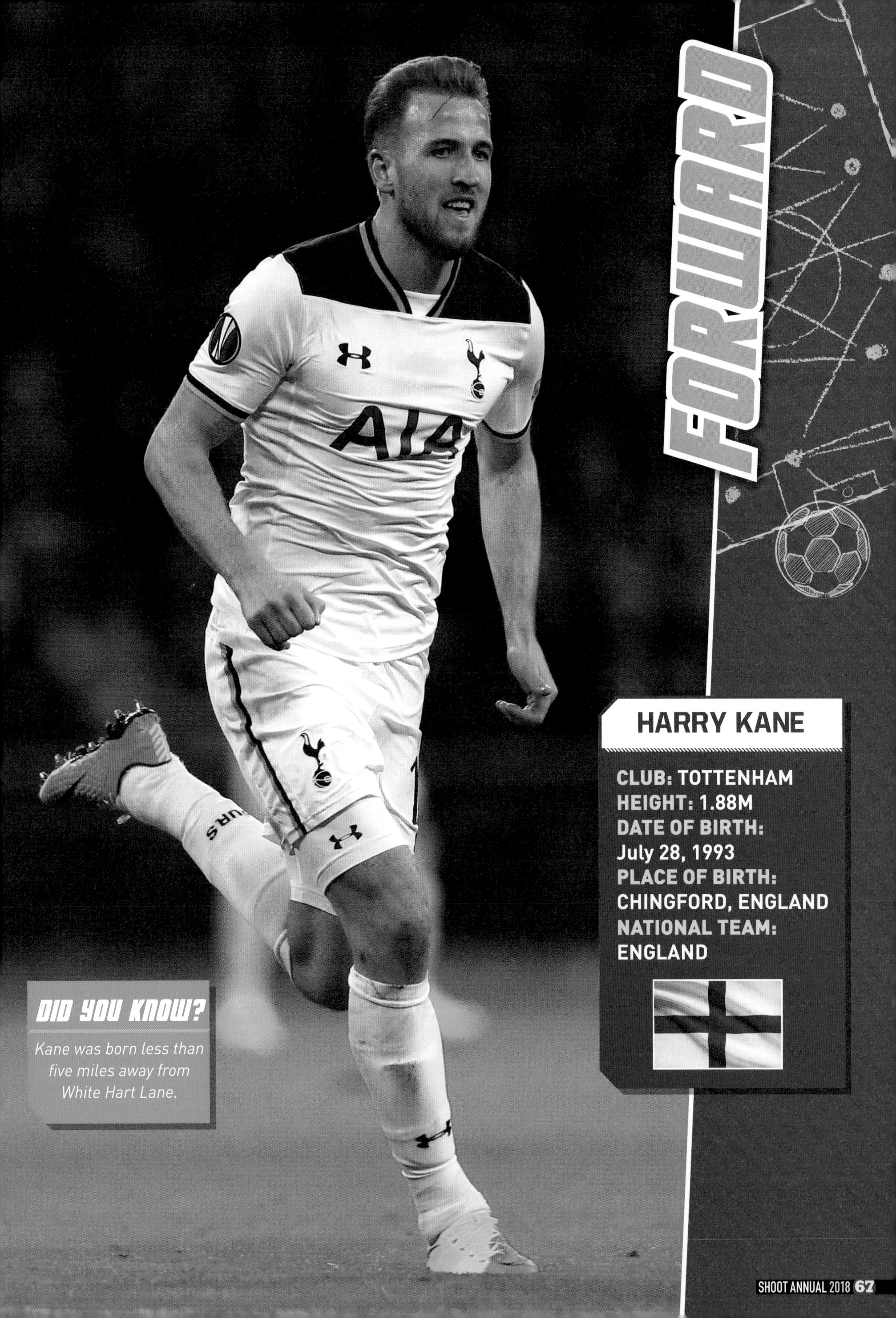

HARRY KANE

CLUB: TOTTENHAM
HEIGHT: 1.88M
DATE OF BIRTH:
July 28, 1993
PLACE OF BIRTH:
CHINGFORD, ENGLAND
NATIONAL TEAM:
ENGLAND

DID YOU KNOW?

Kane was born less than five miles away from White Hart Lane.

CHAMPIONS CROSSWORD

Can you name these 10 Premier League winners in our Champions Crossword? Read each clue to help you fill in each star's surname in our criss-cross puzzle.

DOWN

1. The Premier League's all-time leading goalscorer
2. Manager of Leicester City during the 2015-16 season
3. Chelsea's all-time leading goalscorer
5. Former Arsenal, Barcelona and New York Red Bulls striker
6. Manager often nicknamed the 'Special One'

ACROSS

4. Former Manchester United midfielder's nickname was 'Golden Balls'
7. Captain of Arsenal's 2003-04 'Invincible' squad
8. Manager who lifted the 2016-17 trophy in his debut campaign in English football
9. Manager of Blackburn Rovers during the 1994-95 season
10. Father-son goalkeeping stars who have both lifted the title

SPOT THE DIFFERENCE

Take a close look at these two images of Manchester United celebrating their 2017 EFL Cup final victory. They may look similar, but *SHOOT* has meddled with Photo B! Can you find the 10 differences we have made? Circle each one you spot.

A

B

10 THINGS YOU DIDN'T KNOW ABOUT...

Gab

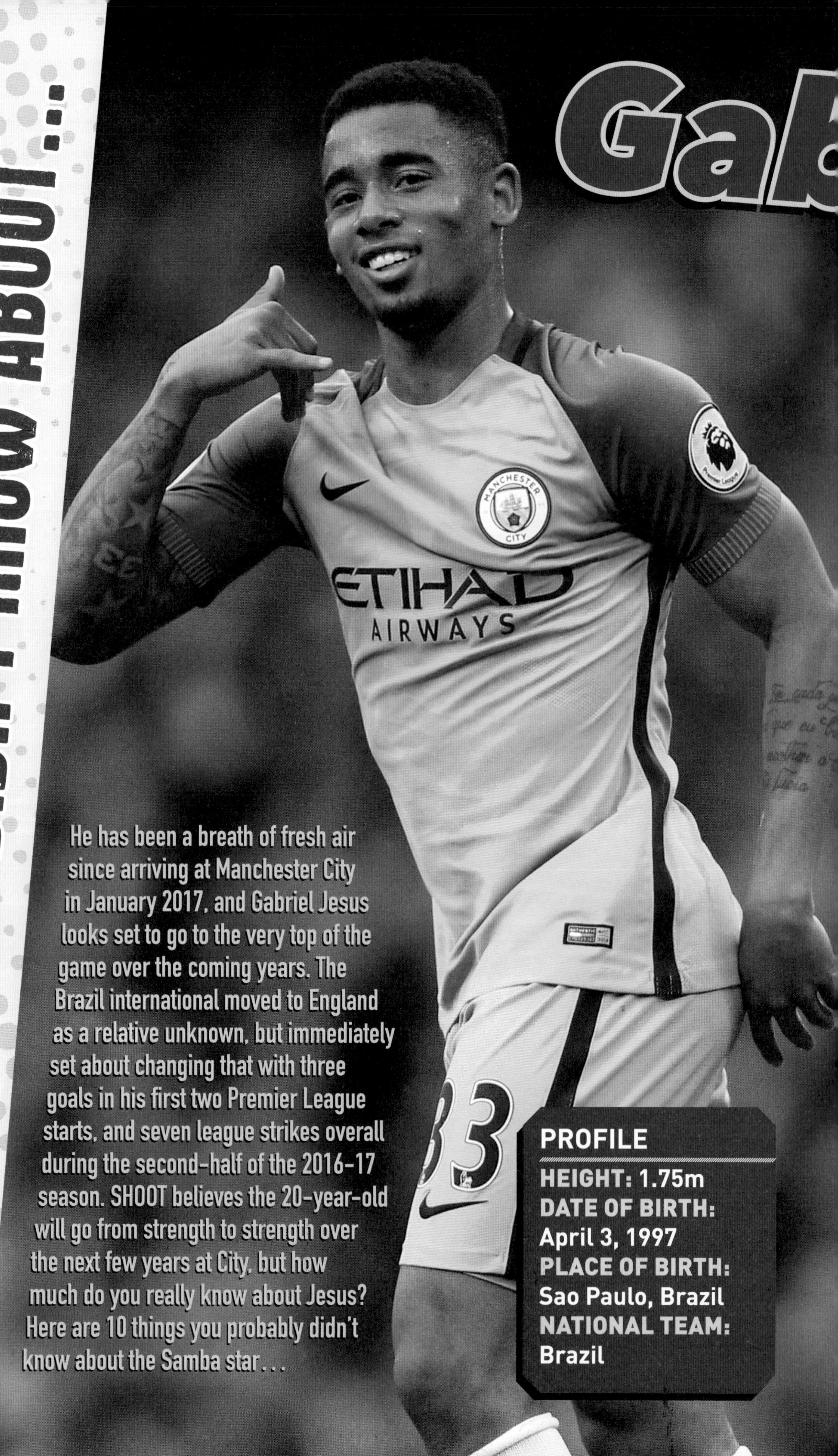

He has been a breath of fresh air since arriving at Manchester City in January 2017, and Gabriel Jesus looks set to go to the very top of the game over the coming years. The Brazil international moved to England as a relative unknown, but immediately set about changing that with three goals in his first two Premier League starts, and seven league strikes overall during the second-half of the 2016-17 season. SHOOT believes the 20-year-old will go from strength to strength over the next few years at City, but how much do you really know about Jesus? Here are 10 things you probably didn't know about the Samba star...

PROFILE

HEIGHT: 1.75m
DATE OF BIRTH: April 3, 1997
PLACE OF BIRTH: Sao Paulo, Brazil
NATIONAL TEAM: Brazil

riel Jesus

1. He trained at a military prison with his amateur team, Little Wonders of the Environment, when he was younger.

2. Jesus burst onto the scene with Palmeiras in his homeland when he signed a youth contract back in 2013, before scoring 54 goals in 48 games in his debut season.

3. His mother is his biggest fan and regularly checks that Jesus has finished his banana and oat smoothie before matches – they help to avoid cramps!

4. Jesus and Brazil team-mate Neymar have a matching tattoo of a young boy playing football in the streets.

5. He turned down more lucrative deals to sign for Manchester City, stating that he wanted to play under manager Pep Guardiola.

6. Jesus rose to fame very quickly and was rewarded with the prestigious Bola de Ouro award in 2016, a Brazilian honour the likes of Neymar, Ronaldinho, Zico and Kaka have previously won.

7. He scored twice on his senior international debut for Brazil in September 2016 – a feat not even the likes of Ronaldo, Ronaldinho, Pele, Zico or Neymar achieved.

8. Manchester City manager Guardiola compared Jesus to a watermelon after netting his first goal for the club, saying, "You have to open to see if it's good or not".

9. Jesus wears the No.33 shirt as a tribute to Jesus Christ – the age when he was crucified.

10. His trademark goal celebration is to pretend to ring his mother.

CLUB SHARERS

Can you figure out all 19 football clubs in *SHOOT's* Club Sharers puzzle? The players surrounding each answer have all played for that side at some stage in their career. Good luck!

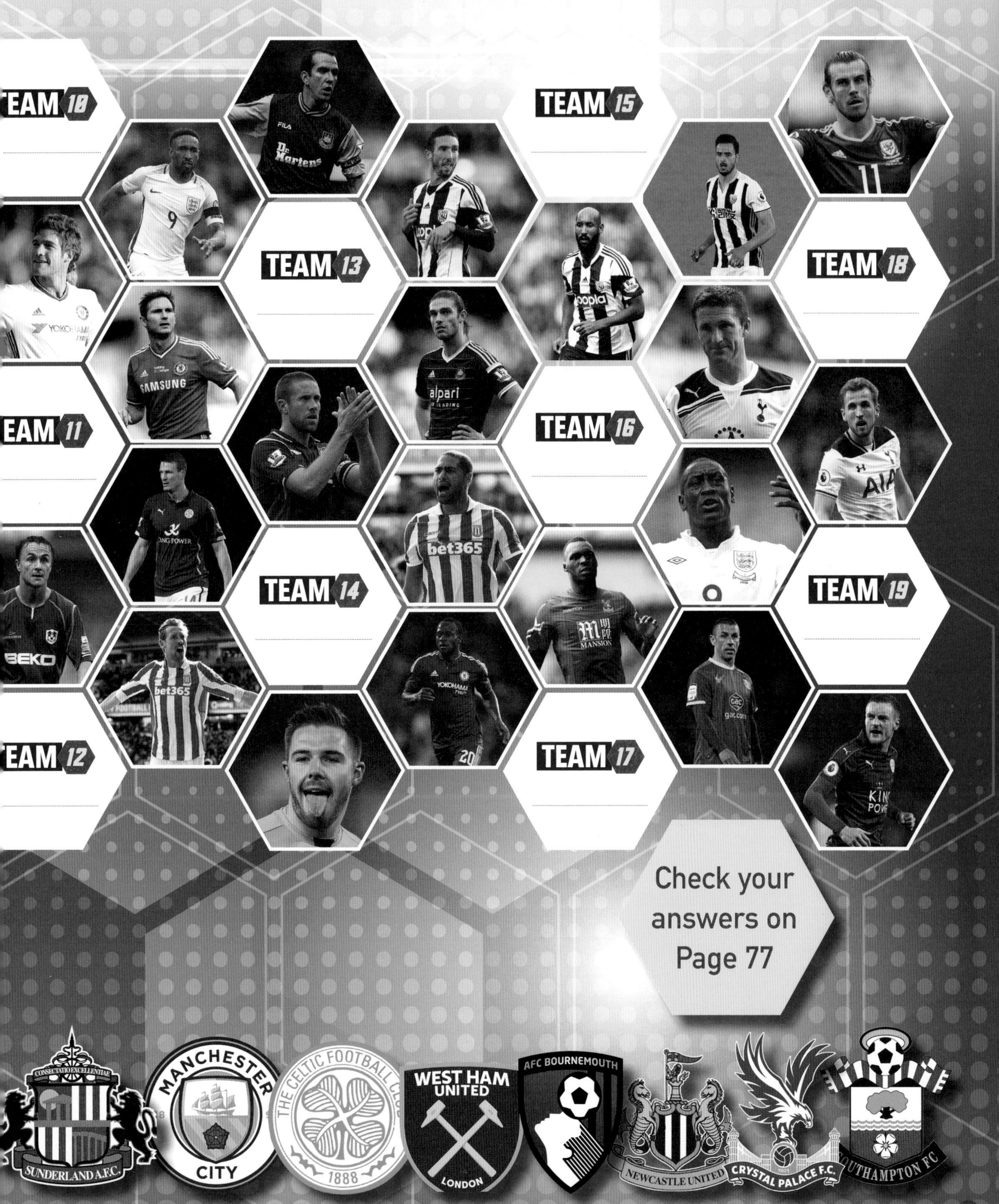

Check your answers on Page 77

FOOTBALLING FAMILIES

Alex and Darren Ferguson

Everyone knows about Sir Alex Ferguson's incredible spell as manager of Manchester United, winning 13 Premier League titles, five FA Cups, and two UEFA Champions League crowns among many more honours. Yet, few know of the achievements of his son, Darren. He is a former professional footballer, most notably for spending eight years at Wrexham between 1999 and 2007, and like his father, is now a manager. The 45-year-old led Peterborough United to back-to-back promotions to the Championship in 2008 and 2009, before returning to London Road to win the League One play-offs in 2011. Darren is now boss at Doncaster Rovers having led them to automatic promotion from League Two in 2017.

Yaya and Kolo Toure

The forenames used for a comical chant belted out around global sporting venues, the Toure brothers of Yaya and Kolo have achieved much in the game, and are continuing to do so. Manchester City midfielder Yaya moved to England back in 2010 after a hugely successful spell with Barcelona, and became an integral part of The Citizen sides that won the Premier League in 2012 and 2014. His brother Kolo was also part of that City squad that lifted the club's first-ever Premier League title, although he tasted previous top-flight triumph with Arsenal during their 2003-04 'Invincible' campaign. The defender moved north of the border to Celtic in the summer of 2016 after a short spell at Liverpool, helping former Reds boss Brendan Rodgers lead his side to a record-breaking Scottish Premiership title in 2017.

Eden and Thorgan Hazard

Many English football fans know of Chelsea winger Eden Hazard, but very few are aware that he has a brother, Thorgan, who has been playing his trade in Germany. However, he did play for Chelsea not long after his elder sibling moved from Lille in 2012, and where Eden has gone on to become one of the best players the Premier League has ever seen, Thorgan unfortunately never made the mark at Stamford Bridge. He did not make a single first-team appearance for The Blues between 2012 and 2015, before signing permanently for Borussia Monchengladbach. With fellow siblings Kylian playing in Hungary and Ethan in the youth academy of Belgian outfit AFC Tubize, where the previous three all played in the early stages of their careers, the Hazards are a supremely talented family of footballers destined for big things.

Football really is a family affair. From fathers and sons to brothers and uncles, there are so many football family stories in the beautiful game today, and throughout the years. Be it the Charlton brothers teaming up to help England win the FIFA World Cup in 1966, to the Toures becoming the feature of a song sung on the terraces around the globe, family affairs are everywhere and thus deserve celebrating. *SHOOT* has picked out several family affairs in and around the British game to honour those fathers, sons, and brothers who are making a name for themselves in the world of football.

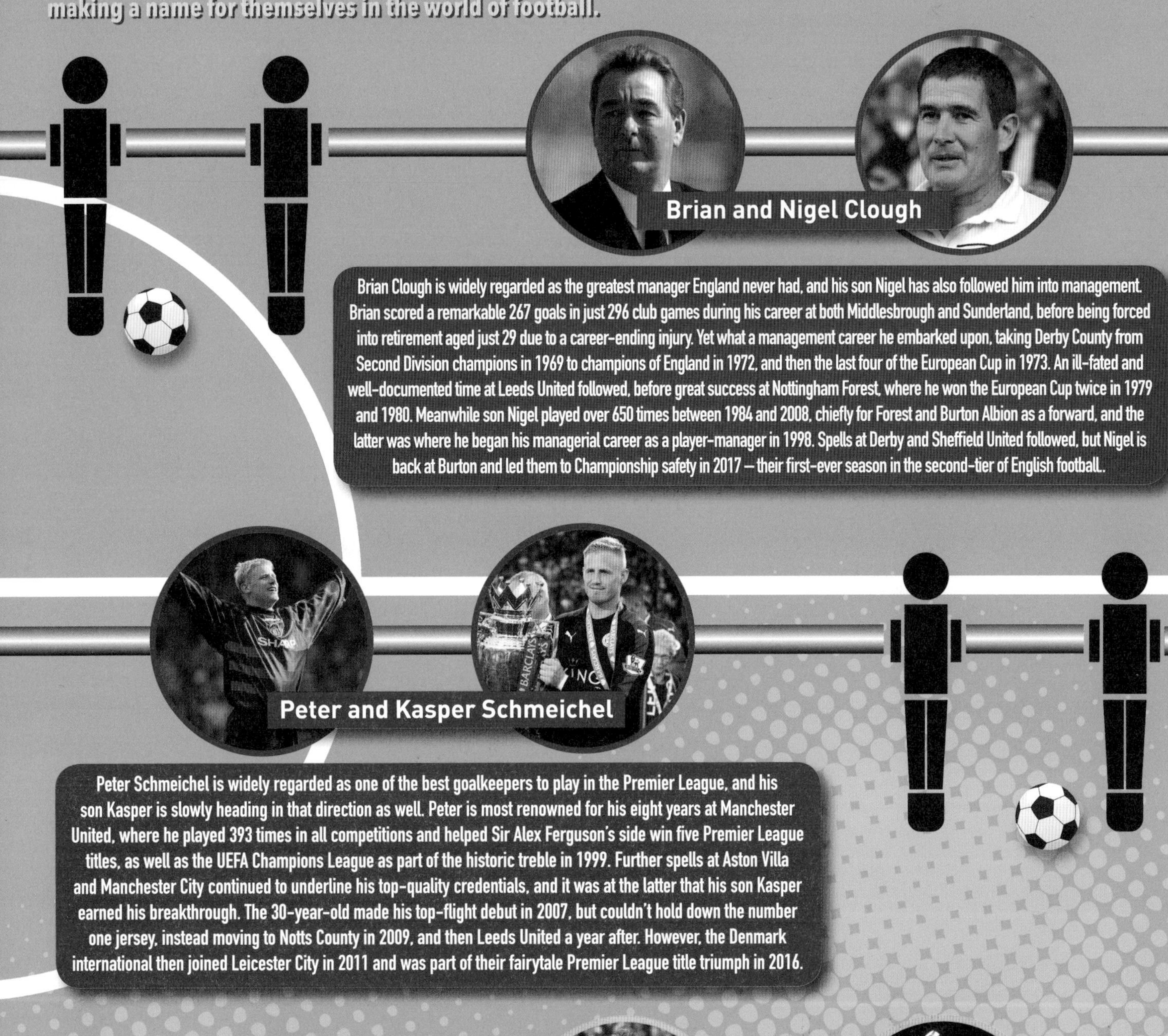

Brian and Nigel Clough

Brian Clough is widely regarded as the greatest manager England never had, and his son Nigel has also followed him into management. Brian scored a remarkable 267 goals in just 296 club games during his career at both Middlesbrough and Sunderland, before being forced into retirement aged just 29 due to a career-ending injury. Yet what a management career he embarked upon, taking Derby County from Second Division champions in 1969 to champions of England in 1972, and then the last four of the European Cup in 1973. An ill-fated and well-documented time at Leeds United followed, before great success at Nottingham Forest, where he won the European Cup twice in 1979 and 1980. Meanwhile son Nigel played over 650 times between 1984 and 2008, chiefly for Forest and Burton Albion as a forward, and the latter was where he began his managerial career as a player-manager in 1998. Spells at Derby and Sheffield United followed, but Nigel is back at Burton and led them to Championship safety in 2017 – their first-ever season in the second-tier of English football.

Peter and Kasper Schmeichel

Peter Schmeichel is widely regarded as one of the best goalkeepers to play in the Premier League, and his son Kasper is slowly heading in that direction as well. Peter is most renowned for his eight years at Manchester United, where he played 393 times in all competitions and helped Sir Alex Ferguson's side win five Premier League titles, as well as the UEFA Champions League as part of the historic treble in 1999. Further spells at Aston Villa and Manchester City continued to underline his top-quality credentials, and it was at the latter that his son Kasper earned his breakthrough. The 30-year-old made his top-flight debut in 2007, but couldn't hold down the number one jersey, instead moving to Notts County in 2009, and then Leeds United a year after. However, the Denmark international then joined Leicester City in 2011 and was part of their fairytale Premier League title triumph in 2016.

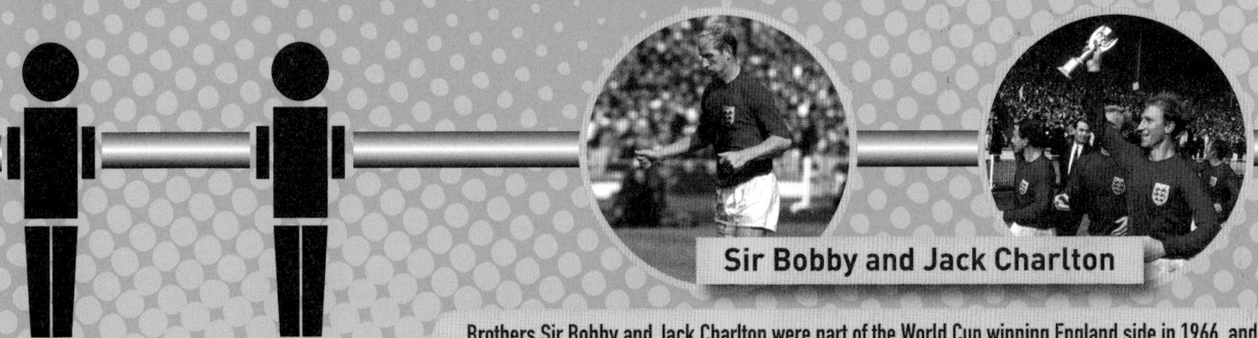

Sir Bobby and Jack Charlton

Brothers Sir Bobby and Jack Charlton were part of the World Cup winning England side in 1966, and will go down in history as two of the greatest players to have ever played for their respective clubs, Manchester United and Leeds United. Sir Bobby, was until January 2017, United's all-time record goalscorer with a remarkable 249 goals in his 758 appearances for The Red Devils, in which time he won three First Division titles, the European Cup and the Ballon d'Or in 1966. While Sir Bobby is widely held as one of the greatest attackers of all-time, his brother Jack is held in high esteem for his defensive abilities. The former centre-half spent his entire club career at Leeds, making his debut in 1953 and going onto appear a further 761 times for the Yorkshire outfit before retiring in 1973, when he turned his attention to management, which included stints in charge of Sheffield Wednesday and the Republic of Ireland.

YOU'VE AGED WELL!

Can you name these past and present international players from these old photos?

1

2

3

4

5

6

ANSWERS

1. Kenny Dalglish 4. David Beckham
2. Danny Welbeck 5. Sol Campbell
3. Robbie Keane 6. Gareth Bale

PAGES 12-13 SPOT THE BALL

Picture 1. D12
Picture 2. C8
Picture 3. C11
Picture 4. B5

PAGE 17 WORDSEARCH

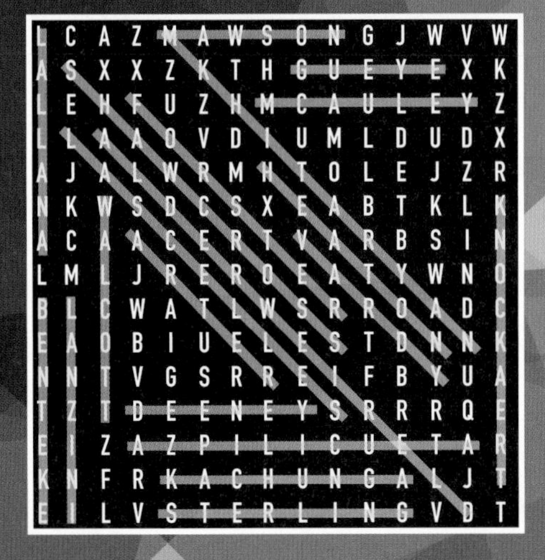

PAGES 22-23 MEGA QUIZ FIRST-HALF

1. Chris Coleman
2. Aaron Ramsey
3. Turf Moor
4. Rangers
5. Harry Kane
6. Huddersfield Town
7. N'Golo Kante
8. Brazilian
9. Ajax
10. 1-4
11. Fara Williams
12. Arsenal
13. Russia
14. Barcelona
15. Granit Xhaka (Arsenal)
16. The Blades
17. League One
18. Alan Shearer
19. 2003-04
20. Burton Albion

PAGE 33 FUNNY FACES

A. HAIR-Paul Pogba
EYES-Peter Crouch
MOUTH-Jill Scott

B. HAIR-Steph Houghton
EYES-Eniola Aluko
MOUTH-Joe Ledley

C. HAIR-Petr Cech
EYES-Ross Barkley
MOUTH-Raheem Sterling

PAGES 36-37 SPOT THE BOSS

PAGES 48-49 STADIUM QUIZ

1. Wembley Stadium - Tottenham Hotspur - 90,000
2. Old Trafford - Manchester United - 75,643
3. London Stadium - West Ham United - 66,000
4. Emirates Stadium - Arsenal - 60,432
5. Celtic Park - Celtic - 60,411
6. Etihad Stadium - Manchester City - 55,097
7. Anfield - Liverpool - 54,074
8. St James' Park - Newcastle United - 52,405

PAGES 60-61 MEGA QUIZ SECOND-HALF

1. Belgium
2. Thibaut Courtois
3. 1966
4. Germany
5. AS Monaco
6. Bradford City
7. Liverpool
8. Southampton
9. Manolo Gabbiadini
10. Danish
11. Jose Holebas (Watford)
12. Watford
13. Everton
14. The Black Cats
15. David Healy
16. Seven
17. Middlesbrough
18. Lincoln City
19. Luton Town
20. Loftus Road

PAGE 68 CHAMPIONS CROSSWORD

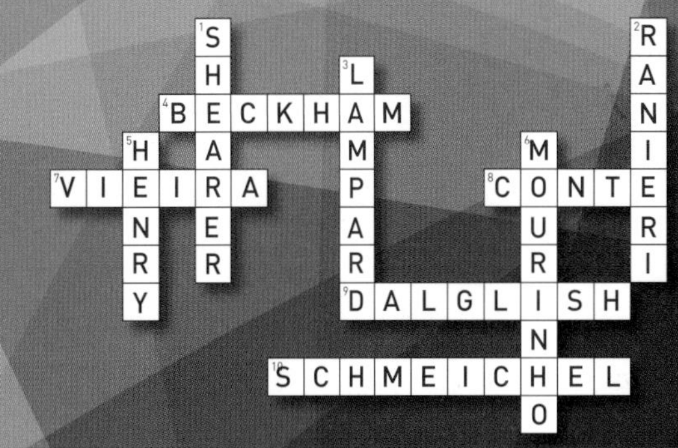

PAGE 69 SPOT THE DIFFERENCE

PAGES 72-73 CLUB SHARERS

1. Everton
2. Man City
3. Leeds Utd
4. Aston Villa
5. Man Utd
6. Celtic
7. Newcastle Utd
8. Arsenal
9. AFC Bournemouth
10. Sunderland
11. Chelsea
12. Southampton
13. West Ham
14. Stoke City
15. West Brom
16. Liverpool
17. Crystal Place
18. Tottenham
19. Leicester City